I0820233

AMERICA
CELEBRATES

First published in 2026 by becker&mayer! kids,
an imprint of The Quarto Group,
142 West 36th Street, 4th Floor,
New York, NY 10018, USA
(212) 779-4972
www.Quarto.com

EEA Representation, WTS Tax d.o.o.,
Žanova ulica 3, 4000 Kranj, Slovenia.
www.wts-tax.si

10 9 8 7 6 5 4 3 2 1

ISBN: 978-0-7603-9860-9

Digital edition published in 2026
eISBN: 978-0-7603-9861-6

Library of Congress Control Number: 2025941361

Publisher: Rage Kindelsperger
Creative Director: Laura Drew
Managing Editor: Cara Donaldson
Editor: Sarah O'Connor
Art Direction and Cover Design: Beth Middleworth
Interior Design: Raine Rath
Author Photo: Ariel Moore
Cover Illustrations: Manu Cunhas
Interior Illustrations pages 4, 6, 12, 26, 54, and 136 by Manu Cunhas

Printed in Malaysia PCA122025

Lexile®: 1110L

AMERICA CELEBRATES

THE MOST INCREDIBLE AND INFLUENTIAL PEOPLE, PLACES & EVENTS OF THE LAST 250 YEARS

Aubre Andrus

b&m! kids

NATIONAL
PARK
SERVICE
YELLOWSTON
NATIO

Contents

Introduction

July 4, 2026, is the 250th anniversary of the signing of the Declaration of Independence—a historic moment when America became, well, America! Before 1776, America was controlled by England, a country across the Atlantic Ocean, but people in America wanted to make their own rules. So, a group of leaders called the Founding Fathers wrote and signed a document, the Declaration of Independence, that announced to the world that they were breaking free from England and their country would be known as the United States of America. That's why July 4 is known as America's birthday.

This anniversary is known as the "semiquincentennial." "Semi" means "half," "quin" means "five," and "centennial" means "100 years." Put it all together and you get a semiquincentennial! Half of 500 (five times 100) equals 250!

A lot has happened over the course of 250 years. Since our country claimed its independence, America has grown from 13 colonies to 50 states—and became the third largest country in the world. We've had 47 presidencies over four different centuries. In 1776, when everyone traveled on horseback, it would be hard to imagine that one day we'd send a pop star to space—just for fun!

This book captures 250 moments, people, and things that represent the United States of America over the last 250 years. You'll find trailblazers, cool inventions, sports stars, important laws, and more. But it was really hard to pick only 250 facts—impossible, really.

There's so much more to learn about American history than what's in the pages of this book. For example, there are entire libraries dedicated to World War II alone. It can't be captured in just a few paragraphs. *America Celebrates* is meant to inspire curiosity about US history and make you crave more knowledge on different subjects. The hope is also that there will be some delightful surprises along the way. For example, did you know the Girl Scouts invented s'mores in 1927?

As you flip through the pages of this book, here are some questions you can ask yourself:

- **Did this person's actions or beliefs change the way people thought about an important issue? Does it change your beliefs or the way you live your life?**
- **If this event did not happen or this person was never born, would our country's history be different? How?**
- **How would your life have been different if you were living during an earlier moment in history?**
- **What people, places, or events have we missed that you think should be included?**
- **What do you think America's future holds—in the next ten years, 100 years, or 250 years?**

Learning about the past can help us better understand our present, which means we can then shape a better future for everyone. There are tough moments in history that may be challenging to read about, but these moments are important because they teach us important lessons for the future. Alongside challenging times in American history are influential people doing incredible things, game-changing technologies that make life easier, and important places in the United States that inspire awe. All together, these 250 moments make up a piece of US history—and that's cause for celebration. Enjoy *America Celebrates* and don't forget to say, "Happy birthday!" to America on the Fourth of July!

There's so much to learn in *America Celebrates*! From the Founding Fathers to space exploration, this book includes so many people and moments that are both serious and fun. Here is a sneak peek of what's to come.

Benjamin Franklin is on the $100 bill, which is why $100 bills are sometimes called "Benjamins."

George Washington is the only president who never lived in the White House or in Washington, DC.

Noah Webster thought the letter "a" should be removed from words like "leather" and "feather" in America's first dictionary since it didn't serve a phonetic purpose (meaning you can't hear the letter when you say the word). His idea didn't catch on—not in 1828 and not today!

Everglades National Park in southern Florida is the only place on the planet where you can find both crocodiles and alligators living together because there's a mix of fresh water from Lake Okeechobee and salt water from the ocean.

Established in 1850, **Los Angeles County** has the highest population in the nation. More people live here than in 40 of the 50 US states.

Alexander Graham Bell thought "Ahoy!" was the best way to answer the telephone, which he invented in 1876, but his rival Thomas Edison popularized "Hello" instead.

The Pixar movie *Cars* is based on a new highway that takes customers away from the small town of Radiator Springs off **Route 66**, which stretched from Illinois to California.

While waiting for a **COVID-19** vaccine to arrive, schools around the country shut down for the rest of the year in the spring of 2020. Students (from kindergarten to college) began learning virtually from their home computers.

Football players that win the final championship game score Super Bowl rings, which cost $30,000 to $50,000, that are usually gold with diamonds and other gems that represent the team's colors.

America the Beautiful

UNITED STATES
Lake Superior
Lake Huron
Lake Michigan
Lake Ontario
Lake Erie
Ottawa
MAINE
Bangor
Augusta
Montpelier
Portland
VERMONT
N. HAMP.
Concord
MASS.
Boston
Providence
RHODE I.
Hartford
CONNECT.
NEW YORK
Burlington
Syracuse
Albany
Springfield
Buffalo
Scranton
New York
Trenton
NEW JERSEY
PENNSYLVANIA
Harrisburg
Philadelphia
Pittsburgh
Baltimore
Dover
DELAWARE
Annapolis
Washington
MARYLAND
40°N
MICHIGAN
WISCONSIN
Green Bay
Milwaukee
Madison
Duluth
St Paul
Grand Rapids
Lansing
Detroit
Chicago
Toledo
Cleveland
Fort Wayne
OHIO
Columbus
Ames
Cedar Rapids
Des Moines
Peoria
ILLINOIS
Springfield
INDIANA
Indianapolis
Cincinnati
WEST VIRGINIA
Charleston
VIRGINIA
Richmond
Virginia Beach
Norfolk
Kansas City
St Louis
Jefferson City
MISSOURI
Evansville
Louisville
Frankfort
Lexington
Owensboro
KENTUCKY
Springfield
Poplar Bluff
Greensboro
Raleigh
Winston-Salem
Nashville
Knoxville
Asheville
NORTH CAROLINA
Charlotte
Wilmington
Fayetteville
Fort Smith
TENNESSEE
Memphis
ARKANSAS
Little Rock
Pine Bluff
Greensville
Chattanooga
Greenville
Columbia
SOUTH CAROLINA
Charleston
Hunstville
Birmingham
Atlanta
Augusta
ALABAMA
Macon
Savannah
Shreveport
Meridian
Jackson
Montgomery
GEORGIA
MISSISSIPI
Mississippi River
Ohio River
LOUISIANA
Baton Rouge
New Orleans
Biloxi
Mobile
Tallahassee
Jacksonville
Gainesville
Daytona Beach
Orlando
Tampa
FLORIDA
Lake Okeechobee
Miami
Key West
Nassau
THE BAHAMAS
ATLANTIC OCEAN
30°N
90°W
80°W

1700–1799

Building America

1 Chief Powhatan: New Neighbors

John Smith, along with other colonists from England, arrived in America in 1607. Colonists are people who leave one country to settle in a new place but still follow the rules of their original country. They were seeking the "New World," which was what people from Europe called the Americas. Although it was new to them, it wasn't actually new—Native Americans had been living in this area for at least 12,000 years.

Captain Smith was a leader of the new settlement, which his people named Jamestown. One day when he was out exploring, Native Americans captured him. But the thing is—he was on *their* land.

Chief Powhatan was the Native American leader of Tsenacomoco (say Sen-uh-co-mo-co), now what we call the state of Virginia. Chief Powhatan was a clever leader who had already united tens of thousands of people across more than 30 tribes and 150 different towns. The tribes followed his orders and delivered food and clothing to his home in the capital city of Werowocomoco (say Wear-o-wo-co-mo-co).

After getting to know each other, the two leaders ended up friends, even though Chief Powhatan spoke Algonquian (a Native American language) and Captain Smith spoke English. The English people who arrived with Captain Smith had no food and needed help. Chief Powhatan and his daughter Pocahontas delivered food as a sign of peace, which helped save Jamestown during a long winter. The Powhatan people went on to trade corn for English resources, like metal, tools, and guns.

With help from the local tribes, Jamestown survived until the next ship of colonists and supplies arrived in the spring of 1609. Without Chief Powhatan and the Native Americans, America wouldn't be what it is today.

The Mayflower: A Journey on the High Seas

In the summer of 1620, a group of Europeans, who we know now as pilgrims, hoped to start a new life and a new church in the New World. Pilgrims are a type of colonist whose main reason for coming to the Americas was to break away from the Church of England.

They boarded the *Mayflower* and the *Speedwell* and set sail from England—but the *Speedwell* sprung leaks. So, everyone squeezed onto the *Mayflower*. Thanks to the delay, the *Mayflower* now had to cross the Atlantic Ocean during storm season.

The passengers spent 66 horrible days at sea—constantly seasick—until they finally arrived in modern-day Massachusetts at a Native American settlement called Patuxet. They named their new home Plymouth, after the town they had departed from in England.

Thanks to the native Wampanoag people, half of the pilgrims survived the winter. In the fall of 1621, the pilgrims celebrated their first successful harvest with the Wampanoag people, which is now known as the first Thanksgiving.

The Thirteen Colonies: Before the States

It took more than 100 years to establish the 13 colonies after Jamestown in 1607. The New England colonies were made up of New Hampshire, Massachusetts, Rhode Island, and Connecticut. The "middle colonies" included New York, Pennsylvania, New Jersey, and Delaware. Finally, the southern colonies included Maryland, Virginia, North Carolina, South Carolina, and Georgia. Each colony had different types of people, jobs, religions, and rules.

King James I saw the New World as a business opportunity for England. He ruled the colonies and sent colonists there to search for gold, plant crops (like tobacco and rice), and collect resources (like trees and fish).

The First School: No Girls Allowed

The Boston Latin School was opened in the city of Boston and the colony of Massachusetts on April 23, 1635. It was the first public school in what would become the United States. When it opened, classes were taught at the house of the headmaster, or main teacher, until the schoolhouse was built in 1645. Five men who signed the Declaration of Independence attended this boys-only school, like John Hancock, Samuel Adams, and Benjamin Franklin. It's still open today, but in a new location where both boys and girls can attend. A Benjamin Franklin statue marks where the original schoolhouse once stood, even though Benjamin Franklin dropped out!

Blackbeard: Pirates in Charlestown

Avaste ye! A notorious pirate named Blackbeard committed his boldest act at the port of Charleston, South Carolina. Pirates steal for a living and sail the high seas with their crewmates, cannons, and swords. In January of 1718, Blackbeard blockaded Charlestown's port, which means the crew stopped people and goods from coming and going. They stole goods and medicine and held prisoners in exchange for money.

Fun Fact: To make his enemies fear him, Blackbeard put the lit fuses of matches under his hat and in his long, black beard during battle. He braided his beard with ribbon too.

The Oldest Library: 45 Books Total

The Darby Free Library in Pennsylvania is the oldest continuously operating library in America. It was created in 1743 when a group of farmers and merchants decided to pool their money together to buy 45 books from London. The books, which ranged from science books to fiction books to a dictionary, were kept at the librarian's home until the town could raise enough money for a library building in 1872. Anyone who returned a book late had to pay a fine: three to six pence (British pennies).

Boston Tea Party: Tea Overboard!

In the middle of the night on December 16, 1773, a group of American colonists disguised as Mohawk Indians boarded three British ships. The *Dartmouth*, *Beaver*, and *Eleanor* were delivering 342 chests of British tea to be sold in America. The colonists threw the entire shipment—92,000 pounds (48 tons) of tea—overboard, filling Boston Harbor with ruined tea leaves.

The colonists who planned this event were members of the Sons of Liberty, a secret political group that opposed the Tea Act, which allowed Britain to tax tea in America. This tax meant colonists had to pay a few cents extra every time they bought tea, and that money went to Britain. The colonists were angry that the British government could make rules like this, especially when no colonists were involved in making these decisions. They called it "taxation without representation."

This event, which we now call the Boston Tea Party, was the first major act of rebellion from the American colonists against the British government, and it's one of the major moments that sparked the American Revolution. You can visit replicas of the *Dartmouth*, *Beaver*, and *Eleanor* today in the Boston Harbor, and there's even a reenactment of the Boston Tea Party every year on its anniversary.

8 The First Museum: Meet the Rattlesnake

Built in 1773, the Charleston Museum in South Carolina is known as America's first museum. It was founded by the Charleston Library Society, a group of men who were interested in studying the natural history of South Carolina. They were likely inspired by the British Museum in London.

The founders asked people from around South Carolina to send them "animals, vegetables, or minerals" unique to the colony as well as any information about those items. Exhibits included exciting scientific discoveries like shells, plants, birds, and animals that didn't exist in England—like the rattlesnake!

The museum went on to display items from around the world since Charleston was a port city where international ships docked with interesting goods. Curious science-lovers from other colonies traveled to the museum too.

9 Paul Revere: The British Are Coming!

On April 18, 1775, Paul Revere was told a secret: Spies had learned that British soldiers were on the move to steal and destroy weapons in Concord, Massachusetts. With no cars or phones, he got on his horse.

Revere was a member of the Sons of Liberty, the secret organization who fought for the rights of the 13 colonies. With other Sons of Liberty, Revere rode toward Concord and through Lexington, stopping at all the houses along the way to share the news that the British were coming.

The colonists where prepared when the British arrived. No one knows who fired the first shot, but the British and American colonists fought the Battle of Lexington and Concord. The colonists won—and the Revolutionary War officially began.

10 George Washington: Father of the Country

George Washington is known as the "father of his country" for many reasons: for leading America to victory against Britain during the Revolutionary War, for helping to establish the Constitution, and for becoming America's first president.

Washington was born in the colony of Virginia in 1732. Shortly after the Revolutionary War began in 1775, Washington was appointed commander of the Continental Army—the 20,000 American soldiers who were fighting to break free from British rule.

Even though the British Army, also called the "redcoats," had more supplies and better trained soldiers, Washington was smart, strategic, and brave, like when he led the army across the Delaware River for a triumphant battle on December 25, 1776.

Years later, Washington was voted to become the first president of the United States of America. He served two terms from 1789 to 1797, when he defined what it means to be the president of the United States of America.

11 Thomas Jefferson: Declaring Democracy

Thomas Jefferson is best known as the author of the Declaration of Independence and the third president of the United States.

Jefferson was born in 1743 in Virginia and had a long political career representing the colony. He eventually became governor of Virginia during the Revolutionary War. He long believed that the colonies should stay loyal to Great Britain, but after all the taxes from Britain and the outbreaks of violence, his beliefs changed. He even led a one-day hunger strike (a form of protest when someone refuses to eat) in support of the colonies. And in 1776, Jefferson was tasked with writing the Declaration of Independence—the very document that would help the 13 colonies break free from Britain.

Today, you can visit his plantation home, Monticello, in Charlottesville, Virginia. It's known for its unique and beautiful architecture, which was designed by Jefferson himself.

The Declaration of Independence:

Breaking Away from Britain

A year after the Revolutionary War started, it became clear that the colonies could not mend their relationship with Great Britain. The only option was to formally declare independence. The colonies had formed a Continental Congress, which was an American government that represented all the colonies, to deal with matters like this.

Thomas Jefferson was asked to write a draft of this announcement, including the reasons why the colonies no longer wanted to be ruled by King George III. Jefferson also wrote a paragraph that still defines the beliefs of America today:

> ***"We hold these truths to be self-evident; that all men are created equal; that they are endowed by their Creator with certain unalienable rights; that among these are life, liberty, and the pursuit of happiness; that to secure these rights, governments are instituted among men, deriving their just powers from the consent of the governed."***

It took Jefferson less than three weeks to write the document. John Adams and Benjamin Franklin helped edit it, and on July 4, the Continental Congress voted to declare independence. Fifty-six men from across the 13 colonies signed the Declaration of Independence in Independence Hall in Philadelphia, Pennsylvania, which you can visit today.

13 **Benjamin Franklin:** Celebrity & Inventor

Benjamin Franklin is known as one of America's Founding Fathers. At age 70, he was the oldest person to sign the Declaration of Independence. He went on to sign two more important documents that helped form the United States: the Treaty of Paris and the Constitution.

Before he was a politician and before the American Revolution started, Franklin was a famous printer, businessman, inventor, author, and scientist in Philadelphia. Back then, people knew electricity existed, but they didn't understand how it worked. In 1751, Franklin wrote a groundbreaking book called *Experiments and Observations on Electricity*. With this knowledge, he invented the lightning rod with the help of a kite, a key, and some lightning.

Franklin also invented bifocals, which are glasses that let you see both near and far. His personal favorite invention was a musical instrument called the armonica, not to be confused with a harmonica, inspired by the music created when you slide your finger along the edge of a glass of water.

14 **John Hancock:** Please Sign Here

As the president of the Continental Congress, John Hancock was the first to sign the Declaration of Independence after overseeing its creation in 1776. Hancock's signature is the largest signature on the document and very fancy. (So much so that when someone needs a signature today, they might say, "Can I have your John Hancock?")

Hancock was a very rich businessman and a well-known patriot, which meant he believed the colonies should be free from British rule. He lived in Boston, which was considered the center of the movement for freedom. He was often targeted by the British. In 1768, the British boarded one of his ships, the *Liberty*, believing that he was smuggling goods into the colonies to avoid paying taxes. This event is considered one of the first to kick off the American Revolution.

Sybil Ludington: Teenage Paul Revere

Two years after Paul Revere went for his famous ride warning citizens that the British were coming, a New York teenager made a similar epic ride on April 26, 1777. Her name was Sybil Ludington and she was just 16 years old. Ludington's dad, Henry, was a colonel in the militia, which was a group of men who were trained to protect their region.

When the Ludington family learned British troops were on their way to attack nearby in Connecticut, Sybil hopped on her horse, Star, and rode 40 miles (64 km) in the rain to warn others in the Hudson Valley. Her warning helped the Patriots quickly push the British back to the Long Island Sound.

Fourth of July: Party in Philly

One year after the signing of the Declaration of Independence in 1777, Philadelphia marked the occasion with a big city-wide celebration. Decorated ships pulled into the harbor. At 1 p.m., they blasted off 13 cannons from each ship in honor of the 13 colonies, then topped it off with a fireworks display that night.

The tradition quickly spread to other cities around the country. It wasn't until 1870 that Congress officially established Independence Day as a holiday. Today, we celebrate similarly with barbecues and parades. And who could forget the fireworks?

Fun Fact: In 1777, the fireworks were orange, which is the natural color of a mini explosion—not red, white, and blue. Colored fireworks weren't invented for another 60 years.

The Treaty of Paris: War Is Over!

Although the US had declared independence from Great Britain in 1776 with the signing of the Declaration of Independence, the Revolutionary War still raged on.

America's independence wasn't formally recognized until 1783 when the Treaty of Paris was signed. Not only did the US and Britain sign the document, but Spain and France did too. The 13 colonies were now officially recognized by the European countries as the United States of America, a new and independent country. The Revolutionary War finally ended, and British troops returned home.

The Constitution: America's Laws

The Constitution that we know today was not the country's first. In 1777, the Articles of Confederation was the first attempt at creating a document that governed the country, but the Founding Fathers knew it needed a major edit. The government couldn't print money, and the states were fighting about border lines and taxes.

The Constitutional Convention was held in Philadelphia in May of 1787. The delegates at the convention now had to create a completely new government. They debated for three months, and the US Constitution was signed on September 17 of that year. George Washington was the first to sign it, and he would become president soon after.

The Constitution united the 13 different states (which previously had different laws) into one national government. This was very different from the Articles of Confederation, which didn't always require the states to work together. Now, Americans were one people.

The first three articles of the new constitution established the three branches of the government: the legislative branch, which is run by Congress; the executive branch, which is run by the president; and the judicial branch, which is run by the courts.

Twenty-seven amendments have been added to the Constitution. Amendments one through ten are considered the Bill of Rights.

19 Mount Vernon: Before the White House

Mount Vernon was George Washington's personal home in Virginia. It was the home his father built in 1734. Washington lived at Mount Vernon for 45 years, but during Washington's eight years as president, there was no White House. He and his wife Martha lived in various homes in the temporary capital cities of New York and then Philadelphia. The Washingtons were quick to return to Mount Vernon in March of 1797, when Washington's second term came to an end.

Mount Vernon was a working plantation, which is a large farm where enslaved Black people who had been transported overseas from Africa live and work without pay. Thomas Jefferson's home, Monticello, was also a working plantation. This was a common practice throughout Colonial America, especially in the Southern Colonies. President Abraham Lincoln eventually put an end to slavery.

20 Philadelphia: First US Capital

In 1790, just after Washington became the first president, it was decided that Washington, DC, would serve as the first permanent capital of the United States. Southern states had felt threatened by a northern-located capital, so DC's middle location felt like a compromise—but it wasn't ready just yet.

Philadelphia served as the temporary capital for ten years while Washington, DC, was being built. During that time, many Philadelphians tried very hard to keep the capital in Pennsylvania. But in 1800, second US President Adams and his wife Abigail moved into the brand-new White House, and DC became home to the nation's official capital city.

Alexander Hamilton: Establishing the Bank

After the Revolutionary War, Founding Father Alexander Hamilton had his work cut out for him. As the first secretary of the treasury, Hamilton was in charge of the financial success of the new country. There were debts to be paid after the war, and things were costing more and more.

Hamilton came up with an idea to help solve these problems. He wanted to create a national bank. But not everyone loved the idea—especially Thomas Jefferson. Jefferson thought creating a national bank would make the government too powerful. The Bank of the United States first opened in Philadelphia on December 12, 1791. Hamilton's new bank could issue paper money, collect the government's tax money, and pay off any of the country's debts. Today, his portrait appears on the ten-dollar bill.

The Bill of Rights: Know Your Rights

The Constitution outlines the rights of the states and the government, but it didn't mention all the rights of American citizens. The Bill of Rights, passed in 1791, helped fix that. It's the first ten amendments, or changes, to the Constitution, and was written by James Madison. Madison would go on to become the fourth president of the United States in 1808. Some of the amendments include:

- **The First Amendment** grants American citizens the right to free speech. That might be through the news, a protest, or through their religious beliefs and practices.
- **The Second Amendment** covers the right to own a gun.
- **The Sixth Amendment** is the right to a fair and speedy trial for people who have been accused of a crime.
- **The Tenth Amendment** says the government's powers must be listed in the Constitution. If it isn't listed in the Constitution or given to a state, the power belongs to the people.

The US Mint: Making Money

Before the Coinage Act of 1792, Americans were trading different kinds of money also known as currency: British pounds, Spanish milled dollars, and more. It was very confusing. The Coinage Act created the US Mint, a place where coins would be created and distributed, in Philadelphia.

The US Mint made all the coins the same across the country: a copper cent and half cent, a silver dime, a half dime, a quarter, a half dollar, and a dollar. There was also a gold eagle ($10), a half eagle ($5), and a quarter eagle ($2.50). It wasn't until 1909 that a president appeared on a coin: Abraham Lincoln was the first.

The Capitol Building: DC's House of Democracy

On September 18, 1793, George Washington led the first parade in Washington, DC, from the White House construction site to the construction site for the US Capitol building. Washington chose a neoclassical design for the building.

Since then, members of the Senate and House of Representatives have gathered at the Capitol to debate issues and draft laws. The building has over 500 rooms.

Fun Fact: The half-domed shape of the National Statuary Hall in the Capitol has an acoustic effect. When you speak to someone from across the room, it might sound like they're right in front of you!

Abigail Adams: 1st Second Lady & 2nd First Lady

In the early days of this new country, First Lady Abigail Adams had a front row seat—and a lot of smart opinions. She shared these opinions with her husband, John Adams, who signed the Declaration of Independence. Although she lacked a formal education, Abigail served as an advisor throughout her husband's political career.

John Adams was the first vice president and second president, so therefore she was the 1st Second Lady and 2nd First Lady. Abigail Adams was also the mother of the sixth president, John Quincy Adams, which makes her one of only two women to be both a wife and mother to a US president. (Barbara Bush was the second!)

1800–1899

Gold Rushes & Great Ideas

26 1600 Pennsylvania Avenue: The White House Opens

Though President George Washington chose the location and the design of the White House, he passed away before construction was done. The second president, John Adams, moved into 1600 Pennsylvania Avenue in 1800, and every president since has called it home.

The White House was considered the biggest house in the country, but it was hard to fill it. Washington, DC wasn't a big city like New York or Philadelphia, where it was easy to shop, so everything needed to be shipped from far away to the White House.

Fun Fact: It wasn't until 1901 that President Theodore Roosevelt moved in and dubbed it the "White House." (He added electric lights too!) Before that, it was called the "president's palace," the "president's house," or the "executive mansion."

The original White House didn't last long—it was burned down in 1814. President James Madison escaped safely while First Lady Dolley Madison, and some White House employees, helped save important items like an original full-length portrait of President Washington. Days later, Madison hired the original architect to rebuild the White House.

Since then, the White House has changed quite a bit. President Theodore Roosevelt added the two-story West Wing and President William Howard Taft added the Oval Office. President Harry S. Truman ordered a complete reconstruction of the inside of the aging building during the late 1940s after a chandelier almost fell on his wife and a leg of his daughter's piano pierced through the floor.

Today, the White House has a garden, a pool, a one-lane bowling alley, a tennis court, a basketball court, a small movie theater, a game room, and a putting green.

27 Louisiana Purchase: America Doubles in Size

Led by the third president, Thomas Jefferson, the Louisiana Purchase became one of the greatest real estate deals ever made. For just $15 million, the US purchased 828,000 square miles (2.1 million sq km) of land west of the Mississippi River from France in 1803. It doubled the size of the country at the time. The land, which was called the territory of Louisiana, included all or parts of 15 modern-day states and made the US one of the biggest countries in the world.

The Louisiana Purchase became Jefferson's biggest achievement as president. What Jefferson didn't plan for was the fact that this land was already populated by thousands of Native Americans. The Louisiana Purchase changed the West forever and, equally so, the future of Native American communities.

28 Lewis, Clark & Sacagawea: Team of Explorers

With the exciting Louisiana Purchase complete, Meriwether Lewis and William Clark were chosen to explore the new territory with their team of about 40 men. They left Missouri in 1804 and headed up the Missouri River.

They brought gifts, including beads, knives, and colored cloth, for the 50 different Native American tribes they met along the way, including the Chinook, Sioux, and Nez Pierce. They met a French-Canadian man Toussaint Charbonneau and his pregnant Shoshone wife, Sacagawea, in North Dakota. They joined the expedition as interpreters, which meant they agreed to help translate the local languages.

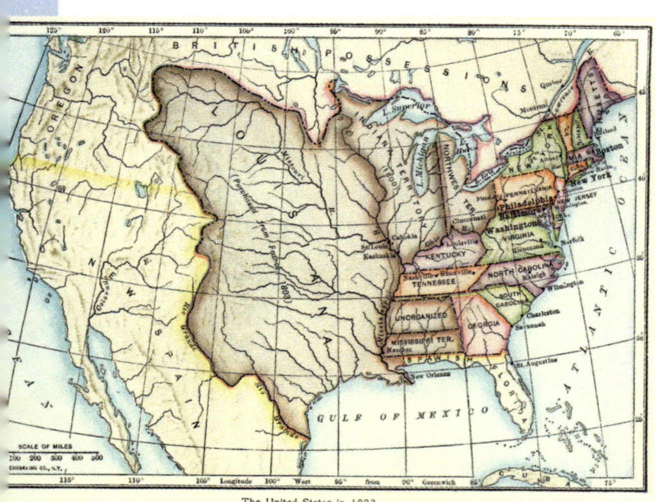

The United States in 1803

Sacagawea gave birth to a son named Baptiste on the expedition. When spring arrived, she strapped her baby on her back and joined the explorers as they voyaged on, traveling at least 15 miles (24 km) per day by foot or by boat. Sacagawea's knowledge of the local language and land proved to be more helpful than they ever imagined.

29 Robert Fulton: Father of the Steamboat

Engineer Robert Fulton did not invent the steam-powered engine, but he had been sketching his idea for a steam-powered boat since he was a boy.

While Fulton's SS *North River* was being built, people called it "Fulton's Folly," because they thought it would fail. When the steamboat left the harbor in New York City for the first time, it was filled with 40 passengers (mostly friends and family). They went to Albany, New York—a 32-hour voyage by steamboat back then. (It would take just two and a half hours by car today!) Fulton ended up being the first to prove that steamboats could be profitable by transporting passengers. He became known as the "father of steam navigation."

30 "The Star Spangled Banner": New American Anthem

One night during a battle amidst the War of 1812 (a war between the United States and Great Britain from 1812 to 1815), amateur poet Francis Scott Key was inspired. Cannons boomed through the night, but as the sun came up, he could see it: The American flag still waved from Fort McHenry. The British had failed.

Key wrote the famous words, "Oh say can you see by the dawn's early light" and named the song "Defence of Fort McHenry." It became an instant hit. One music printer changed the name to "The Star-Spangled Banner." Although it was written in 1814, "The Star Spangled Banner" didn't become the national anthem until 1931.

31 America's First Dictionary: Color, Not Colour

In 1828—at the age of 70—Noah Webster completed the final edition of the *American Dictionary of the English Language*. It took him 22 years to define over 65,000 words, and it was the first time someone compiled an American dictionary. He started the project because Americans were speaking, spelling, and using English words differently than the British did.

For example, Americans spelled "color" while the British spelled "colour." He also added uniquely American words like "skunk" and "squash," plus more words that were unique to America's various natural environments.

32 Maria Stewart: A Woman (Gasp!) Speaks Out

In the 1800s, it was very unusual for women to speak in public—especially Black women. And it was even more unusual for both men and women to sit together in an audience to listen. People thought it was "improper." But on April 28 of 1832, Maria Stewart, a Black activist, took the stage in Boston to a mixed audience of men and women, both Black and white.

An activist is someone who fights for change. Stewart fought for women's rights, and she fought against racism and segregation, two major issues that Black Americans faced during this time.

On that night, Stewart boldly spoke about equality and the importance of freedom for Black people, many of whom were still enslaved at the time in Southern states. She wanted white Americans to join the fight too, not just free Black people.

Stewart went on to open a school in Washington, DC, for the children of enslaved families who were fleeing the Southern states during the Civil War.

33 Oberlin College: First Female Graduates

Oberlin College opened in Ohio in 1833. Both men and women were able to enroll, but women were limited to earning a diploma from a "Ladies Course." That changed in 1837 when four women enrolled in Oberlin College's undergraduate program. In 1841, three of the four women graduated. It was the first time an American college granted women an undergraduate degree.

The college was also the first to admit Black students in 1835. Mary Jane Patterson became the first Black woman to earn a bachelor's degree from an American college in 1862. Just before that, between 1830 and 1860, Oberlin helped about 50,000 people escape from slavery through the Underground Railroad (page 36). They were known as station 99.

34 Oregon Trail: Americans Head West

Now that the country's borders stretched far past the Mississippi River, Americans were eager to travel out West and settle. Lewis and Clark's expedition was a great success, but the group took a rough path and relied on boats. Families could not follow that route with all their belongings.

Fun Fact: Many Native Americans already had settled the American West. Wagon trains on the Oregon Trail often used Pawnee and Shoshone trail guides.

In 1810, a man named Robert Stuart completed a 2,000-mile (3,218 km) and ten-month-long journey from Oregon City, Oregon, to St. Louis, Missouri. His route, now known as the Oregon Trail, was less dangerous than Lewis and Clark's. It weaved through Idaho, Wyoming, Nebraska, and Kansas.

In the spring of 1843, a wagon train—complete with 120 wagons, 1,000 people, and thousands of oxen and cattle—gathered in Missouri. The wagon train began their journey, which is now known as the Great Emigration of 1843, and made it safely to Oregon five months later. The wagons traveled about 15 to 20 miles (24 to 32 km) per day. Each wagon usually included a wooden bed, cargo and supplies, and room to hold people, but it was a bumpy ride and people often walked alongside the oxen-driven wagon or rode a horse.

After the Great Emigration, hundreds of thousands more pioneers followed to settle the new land. The journey was not easy. It was long, and people got sick and sometimes died. Trading posts popped up along the frontier to help supply food and equipment for the five-month journey.

35 Samuel Morse: The Electric Telegraph

In the 1800s, it could take weeks to deliver news using horse-and-carriage mail carts. Samuel Morse was set on changing that.

He (and a group of both English and American researchers) figured out how to transmit electrical signals through a wire that connected two stations. Morse assigned a set of dots and dashes to each letter of the alphabet—what we know today as the Morse code! These series of dots and dashes would spell out letters and eventually sentences.

Fun Fact: .... . .-.. .-.. ---
"Hello" in Morse code!

In 1844, Morse sent the first electric telegraph message from the US Capitol building in Washington, DC, to a railroad station in Maryland. It said, "What hath God wrought!" which was a quote from the Bible. Soon telegraph cables lined the country.

36 Florida & Texas: 28 States & Counting

Florida became the 27th state in the United States on March 3, 1845. It became the state with the longest coastline in the mainland US with 825 miles (1,328 km) of sandy beaches. Today, Florida is home to the world's most visited theme park: Disney World. It's also the site of NASA's rocket launches at Cape Canaveral.

Texas followed shortly after Florida and became the 28th state later that year on December 29. It had formerly been a part of Mexico and then an independent country since 1836. Today, Texas is the second largest state in the US. (Alaska is the first!)

37 **Frederick Douglass:** Author of *An American Slave*

Frederick Douglass wrote three autobiographies about his life as an enslaved person at a time when many enslaved people could not read or write. His first book, *Narrative of the Life of Frederick Douglass, an American Slave,* was an instant bestseller in 1845. American audiences found the story of Douglass's life shocking, and the book helped propel the fight against slavery.

Douglass was born into slavery in Maryland in 1818. He taught himself to read and write, and as a young teenager, he began teaching other enslaved people how to read. He escaped slavery in 1838 and made his way to New York. He started sharing stories about his life. Soon, he became a speaker and a leader of the abolitionist movement, which was in support of ending slavery in America.

With more than 160 portraits, Douglass was the most photographed American of the nineteenth century. He believed that a photograph showed dignity and respect, and he wanted to present himself with as much dignity and respect as any white man of the time. His picture was included in his best-selling autobiography. To further prove himself as a voice for human rights, Douglass founded the *North Star,* a newspaper for Black abolitionists in 1847.

President Abraham Lincoln befriended Douglass and even sat Douglass nearby during his second inauguration speech. The two had an interesting relationship where they listened to and learned from one another. Douglass gave a dedication speech at the Emancipation Memorial in Washington, DC, after Lincoln's death.

38 California Gold Rush: From Rags to Riches

A major discovery at Sutter's Mill in 1848 sparked the largest migration in US history, and it was all for gold. Carpenter James Marshall was building a water-powered sawmill for John Sutter near Coloma, California, when he saw something glittering in the water—gold! The two men had no idea that $2 billion worth of precious metal was lying at the base of the nearby Sierra Nevada Mountains.

Though they tried to keep it a secret, news of gold at Sutter's Mill reached San Francisco first. By summer, most of the men in the city had headed to the mines in the Sacramento Valley to wade through freezing streams. The California Gold Rush had officially begun. The stories were shocking—two miners found $17,000 in gold in just one week.

Fun Fact: One of the mining town shops that opened during the Gold Rush was run by Levi Strauss in San Francisco. He and his partner Jacob Davis received a patent for work pants with metal rivets—what we know today as blue jeans—that became the preferred outfit for 49ers.

It wasn't until the following year that thousands more American and European men—and some women, too—headed west to California for their chance to strike gold. By 1849, there were 100,000 gold-seekers added to the California population. They were nicknamed "49ers" after the year they arrived. That year, $10 million in gold was discovered—and the numbers kept rising from there.

39 Elizabeth Cady Stanton: The Fight for Women's Rights

Elizabeth Cady Stanton, together with Lucretia Mott, held the first women's rights convention in Seneca Falls, New York, in 1848. Three hundred people attended. For the event, Stanton wrote a revised version of the Declaration of Independence, called the "Declaration of Sentiments," which included the word "woman" or "women" throughout. For example, it began with: "We hold these truths to be self-evident; that all men *and women* are created equal."

The declaration also added more ideas that would help empower women, like giving them a formal education, the right to own property, and the right to vote—all ideas that treated men and women as equals. This sparked the women's suffrage movement, which was a nationwide movement supporting the right for women to vote. Stanton's thoughts guided the movement into the next century.

40 Lucretia Mott: Say No to Cotton & Sugar!

Lucretia Mott fought for equality for both Black Americans and women throughout her life. She despised slavery so much that she wouldn't buy cotton or cane sugar—two items that were produced through the unpaid labor of enslaved African and African American people.

When Mott traveled to London to attend the 1840 World Anti-Slavery Convention with her husband, she wasn't allowed inside. At the time, women weren't allowed to sit in an audience full of men or take part in political discussions. Someone else was turned away at the door—Elizabeth Cady Stanton.

This inspired the two abolitionists to create the first women's rights convention where Mott gave the opening and closing speeches at the two-day event. Mott continued to fight for equality for all, including when the 15th amendment was ratified in 1870—it gave Black men the right to vote, but not women.

41 **Harriet Tubman:**

The Underground Railroad's Most Famous "Conductor"

Harriet Tubman was born into slavery, but she successfully escaped to freedom in 1849. She traveled on foot from Maryland to Philadelphia where she landed a job and saved money as a free Black woman. The next year, she made the dangerous trip back to the South to save enslaved friends and family members, including her parents. Over a ten-year period, she returned to Maryland 19 times and led or assisted more than 100 enslaved people to freedom—even though it was illegal and life-threatening.

A $40,000 reward was offered for Tubman's capture. She was one of the most well-known "conductors" on the Underground Railroad, a secret network of hundreds of safehouses, people, and paths that helped enslaved Black people escape to freedom in the North and Canada.

Although it wasn't a literal railroad, volunteers used railroad terminology. "Stations" were safehouses where runaways could rest and get fed. "Stationmasters" ran the safehouses, and "conductors" helped move people from one station to the next. Both Black and white people helped the runaways escape to freedom by providing safety, money, food, clothing, or supplies. During her time as a conductor, Tubman helped newly freed Black people escape to a new home away from slavery and unfair treatment.

42 **California:** America's Produce Capital

The United States acquired the land that became the state of California when the Mexican-American War ended in 1848. California officially became the 31st state on September 9, 1850. Its first capital was San Jose, but that didn't last for long. The California state capital moved to Sacramento in 1854, where it remains today.

Today, when you think of California, you might think of Hollywood, beaches, Disneyland, or national parks (California has nine, more than any other state!). But the state plays an even more important role: California farmers help feed the entire country. California grows a lot of the fresh food that Americans eat every day, like avocados, broccoli, carrots, cauliflower, grapes, kale, kiwis, lemons, peaches, pistachios, raisins, raspberries, and more—as well as milk and cream!

43 **"Bloomers":** Introducing Women to Pants

Amelia Bloomer was a women's rights advocate and the editor of the first women's newspaper, *The Lily*. She focused her efforts on a unique angle: the health and safety effects of women's clothing. At the time, women wore long dresses with corsets (an undergarment that uncomfortably tightened the waist and could make it difficult to breathe). Made up of six to eight layers, a dress could weigh 15 pounds (7 kg), which put stress on women's bodies and made it hard to move around.

Bloomer had learned about "pantaloons," which were a knee-length skirt with loose pants underneath. With her readers, she shared why pantaloons were better for women—and that she would be wearing them moving forward. It was radical at the time for a woman to wear pants! People were appalled, surprised, excited, and angry. *The Lily* went from 400 readers per month to 4,000. Her readers followed her lead by wearing the pantaloons, which soon became known as "Bloomers."

Joseph Leidy's Discovery: Unearthing Dinosaur Fossils

In 1856, paleontologist Joseph Leidy was tasked with studying 75-million-year-old fossilized teeth. They had been discovered in the Judith River region of Montana three years earlier by explorer and paleontologist Ferdinand Vandeveer Hayden. Sometimes it takes years for scientists to analyze and decide just what it was that they've found! Leidy decided three of the eight fossilized teeth were from dinosaurs: *Trachodon*, *Troodon*, and *Deinodon*. That meant these were America's first dinosaur fossils!

Fun Fact: New Jersey named the *Hadrosaurus* its official state dinosaur in 1991, after years of advocating from fourth grade teacher Joyce Berry and her classes at Strawbridge Elementary School in Haddon Township.

Two years later, Leidy went on to identify the first duck-billed dinosaur after analyzing a fossilized dinosaur skeleton similar to an *Iguanodon* but with a flattened jaw. It was uncovered in Haddonfield, New Jersey, so he named it Hadrosaur, a term we still use today. The fossil was also the first well-preserved and almost complete dinosaur fossil found in the United States.

Today, the US is tied with China for having discovered the most dinosaur fossils, with about 320 named species. Almost all of the states have produced at least one dinosaur fossil, but California is the state with the most fossil discoveries. Other popular states for dino digging include Wyoming, Montana, and New Mexico. A visit to the Dinosaur National Monument on the Colorado–Utah border is a chance to see more than 1,500 fossils on display and reconstructed skeletons of *Allosaurus*, *Stegosaurus*, and *Diplodocus*.

The First Elevator in America: Going Up!

In 1857, the Haughwout Department Store in New York City featured something that was never seen in the country before—an elevator! New York was one of the world's largest cities at the time, but the buildings weren't taller than four or five stories.

Before the store installed the elevator to their five-story building, elevators only had been used to transport cargo—never humans. Archimedes invented the first elevator back in 236 B.C. in Ancient Greece—that's almost 2,300 years ago! The lift system was powered by humans who pulled on a rope that was wrapped around a drum to move animals or goods. Haughwout's modern passenger elevator was invented by Elisha Otis. It was powered by a steam engine and moved at a speed of 40 feet (12 m) per minute. (Today's elevators are much faster—they can move 40 feet per second!)

Customers were wary—they refused to use it and worried it wasn't safe. Ultimately, the elevator only lasted three years in the store, but elevators are everywhere today!

Central Park, NYC: First Public Park in America

Before Central Park opened in 1858, the only place New York City residents could wander around and get fresh air was a graveyard! Central Park, located right in the middle of Manhattan, added a much-needed green space and public place for relaxation in the rapidly growing city. The first section of the park—a man-made body of water—opened in the winter of 1858. On Christmas morning that year, 8,000 people took to the ice to try a new hobby: ice skating! The gigantic park was built over the next 15 years.

The land was originally swampy and rocky, so every hill, slope, and forested area was built by hand. Workers moved tons of soil; planted 500,000 trees, shrubs, and vines; and built 36 bridges and arches. Central Park, finally completed in 1876, became iconic and influenced urban parks around the country. It's now a national historic monument. It has 21 playgrounds, a zoo, two ice skating rinks, three small lakes, basketball courts, baseball and soccer fields, and an open-air theater.

47 Abraham Lincoln: Uniting a Divided Nation

When Abraham Lincoln was elected president in 1861, the Southern states were worried. President Lincoln (and most Northern states) opposed slavery, and the Southern states were using the free labor of enslaved African and African American people to run their businesses every day. In 1850, approximately half of the people living in Florida were enslaved.

By early 1861, Florida, South Carolina, and Mississippi seceded from the Union, which means they separated from the North. Eventually, 11 Southern states formed the Confederate States of America and created their own constitution to protect slavery. The Civil War began in April of that year, with Lincoln's main goal being to unite the nation.

During the third year of the war, in January of 1863, Lincoln signed the Emancipation Proclamation—a turning point in the Civil War. It freed millions of enslaved African and African American people in the Confederate states. It became not just a war about the union but a war about freedom.

The Confederacy surrendered on April 9, but just days later on April 14, President Lincoln was killed while watching a play at the Ford's Theatre in Washington, DC. He was shot by John Wilkes Booth, an angry Confederate who hated Lincoln for freeing enslaved people and reuniting the country.

Lincoln is considered the greatest president in history for saving the Union and abolishing slavery. He is the most written-about figure in American history.

48 Gettysburg Address: 272-Word Speech

During the Civil War in November of 1863, President Lincoln delivered one of the most important speeches in American history, the Gettysburg Address. It took place at the newly formed National Cemetery of Gettysburg in Pennsylvania, which was the site of one of the bloodiest and most significant battles of the Civil War in July of 1863.

Lincoln's speech was less than two minutes long—just 272 words—but it has gone down in American history as the most memorized and most quoted speech. He started with the words, "Four score and seven years ago." "Score" means 20, so "87 years ago" when America was founded. The Civil War was a test, Lincoln said, to see whether the United States would last. Lincoln also expressed the importance of the Declaration of Independence, which said that "all men are created equal," as opposed to the Constitution, which didn't prohibit slavery.

Fun Fact: Abraham Lincoln was the tallest president at six feet four inches.

49 13th Amendment: Slavery Is Abolished

Slavery was finally declared illegal across the entire US after the passing of the 13th Amendment in December of 1865. Lincoln's Emancipation Proclamation in 1863 was the first step in the process, but it was technically a wartime document and did not apply to the entire country—just the Southern states.

President Andrew Jackson, who had been vice president to Lincoln but became the 17th president after Lincoln's death, got to work. Now that the Civil War had come to an end, he and Congress knew they needed to pass an official amendment to abolish, or remove, slavery from the country forever and protect the approximately four million African and African American people who had been or still were enslaved. Jackson's first major policy passed, and the US declared slavery illegal 89 years after the country was first formed.

During this time of rebuilding after the war, newly freed Black people had to find jobs and housing while overcoming racism. Black and white teachers from the North and South helped educate the newly freed people.

Little Women: An American Classic Debuts

Novelist Louisa May Alcott's instant success, *Little Women,* is considered the first story about an "all-American girl." The novel features the March sisters Jo, Meg, Beth, and Amy—relatable, strong female characters based on her real-life sisters. (Jo was based on Louisa herself.) Alcott's publisher asked her to write a story for girls, which she didn't want to do. But she figured her and her sister's childhood adventures growing up during the Civil War might be interesting enough to write about.

The first edition of *Little Women* sold out within days. Its popularity remains today. *Little Women* has continuously been sold since its debut in 1868. It went on to be made (and remade) into a movie seven times over (between 1917 and 2019) as well as into different formats: a miniseries, an opera, an anime series, a musical, a ballet, a web series, a Broadway play, and spin-off books.

Little Women remains a feminist (the belief that everyone should be treated equally regardless of their gender) classic today. Alcott is known as an author who supported women's rights through the stories she penned and through her real-life actions. The end of the book was very surprising for its time—it didn't end with a wedding the readers expected. Instead, the main character Jo pursues her dreams of becoming a writer instead of marrying her childhood friend, Laurie.

51 Transcontinental Railroad: Connecting the Coasts

In 1869, the opening of the Transcontinental Railroad transformed America forever. It was the first time the East Coast and West Coast were connected by railway, which opened the country up to everyone. This was a great step forward—before immigrants had to travel by wagon or boat on long, dangerous routes. Now anyone could make the 3,000-mile (4,828 km) journey across the US quickly and safely as long as they had a train ticket.

Such a big project required big sacrifices. For six years, thousands of Irish immigrants, Civil War veterans, and Chinese immigrants built bridges, drilled through mountainsides to create tunnels, and laid train tracks made of steel. It was grueling and dangerous work, and many families were displaced along the route, including Native Americans. When it was done and the final track was laid in the state of Utah, America entered an era of growth, with thousands of immigrants moving west.

52 15th Amendment: Black Men Vote

For Black Americans, the 13th, 14th, and 15th Amendments were huge steps in the right direction—though a lot of work was left to do. While the 13th Amendment set enslaved African Americans free and the 14th Amendment promised them citizenship, it wasn't until the 15th Amendment that Black male citizens were guaranteed the right to vote. Specifically, it said that the right to vote could not be denied because of someone's "race, color, or previous condition of servitude." Women of any race still could not vote at this time. This was a major moment in the fight for civil rights, yet there will still a long road with many challenges facing African Americans.

53 Yellowstone National Park: Protected Land

Before Yellowstone, there were no national parks in the country. In the mid-1800s, people were buying land and building up towns and cities, which could make them more money. The idea of protecting areas for "recreational use" was completely unheard of.

President Abraham Lincoln made the first step toward protecting land for public use when he signed the Yosemite Grant in 1864. It protected California's stunning Yosemite Valley, which included the waterfall Bridalveil Fall and the rock formations Half Dome and El Capitan, plus a nearby grove of giant Sequoias, which are some of the oldest trees on Earth. Many credit Lincoln with coming up with the national park concept.

In 1872, Congress moved to protect another area: Yellowstone, but this time they declared it an official national park. This meant its geysers and hot springs would be for the "enjoyment of the people." No one could buy, build, or settle the land. Its natural beauty, and the wildlife within it, would be protected for generations to come. Protecting the land also meant displacing Native American tribes that lived in the area, who faced extreme challenges and unfair treatment as they desperately tried to cling to their land. At least 27 tribes could no longer hunt, fish, or gather resources on this preserved land.

Today, there are 433 sites that are protected by the National Park Service. That includes 63 national parks, as well as battlefield sites, military parks, and national historic sites ranging from the volcanoes of Hawaii to the Denali Wilderness of Alaska to the Everglades in Florida to Yosemite, which became the third official national park in 1890.

Arbor Day: Nebraska *Really* Loves Trees

Thanks to Nebraska, people around the world celebrate Arbor Day in April every year. Arbor Day was created to encourage Nebraskans to plant trees at a time when the state did not have many. There was even a competition with prizes—whichever county planted the most trees, won! On that first Arbor Day in 1872, Nebraskans planted more than one million trees. The holiday was a dream of newspaper editor J. Sterling Morton, who was passionate about planting trees and lobbied for an official holiday to be declared in his state. By 1907, Arbor Day was celebrated by every state in the US.

Susan B. Anthony: Suffragist

In July of 1876, a 100-year (or centennial) celebration occurred at Independence Hall in Philadelphia. Inside the hall were many men—as well as six unwelcome female members of the National Woman Suffrage Association.

Activist Susan B. Anthony approached the platform and read something out loud: "The Declaration of the Rights for Women of the United States." Anthony said, "We ask justice, we ask equality, we ask that all the civil and political rights that belong to citizens of the United States, be guaranteed to us and our daughters forever." The women scattered copies of the document as they hurried out of the building.

> ***Fun Fact:*** Susan B. Anthony was arrested for voting in a presidential election. The judge found her guilty and fined her $100. She never paid.

Harvey House: Stop for a Bite

Now that train travel was the fastest way to travel across the country, Americans needed somewhere to eat and sleep along the way. Entrepreneur Fred Harvey saw an opportunity. He opened his first Harvey House restaurant along the tracks of the Atchison, Topeka, and Santa Fe Railway in Topeka, Kansas, in 1876. As the railway expanded further west, so did Harvey House. He added more restaurants (and shops and hotels!) along the tracks in New Mexico, Arizona, and California. In doing so, Harvey House became the first restaurant chain in America. His waitresses, the legendary Harvey Girls, became one of America's first all-women workforces.

57 Alexander Graham Bell's Telephone: Hello?

During his life, scientist Alexander Graham Bell secured 18 patents for his inventions. He was fascinated with sound technology, and it may be because his wife and mother were deaf. Bell figured out how to turn electricity into sound, which meant he could now send sound from one place to another. He called his invention an "electrical speech machine." On March 7, 1876, he received a patent for the technology.

Three days later, he made the first phone call to his assistant in the other room. He said, "Mr. Watson, come here. I want to see you." Within months, he proved he could make a phone call across a few miles. Thanks to Bell's technology, we can talk to each other instantly at any time of day all over the world.

58 American Red Cross: Clara Barton to the Rescue

During the Civil War, Clara Barton was known as the "Angel of the Battlefield." A self-taught nurse, she brought food, medical supplies, clothing, and her medical services to wounded soldiers during every major battle. She did this voluntarily—no one asked her. Barton often ventured into dangerous battle sites.

In 1869, Barton visited the International Red Cross in Geneva, Switzerland. The organization was created to train volunteers who could help wounded soldiers during wartime. Twelve European countries had agreed that during wartime, all sick and wounded should be protected and cared for—regardless of what country they came from or what their nationality was. This agreement was called the Geneva Convention.

Fun Fact: Barton loved animals too, especially cats. For her bravery and hard work during the Civil War, a senator gifted Barton a kitten with a bow around its neck.

When Barton returned to the US, she opened the first American branch of the Red Cross in 1881. For the next 20 years, Barton led the American Red Cross. Her branch of the Red Cross provided not only wartime services but also disaster relief to those in need, from sending cornmeal and flour to Russia during a famine in 1892 to distributing over $120,000 in aid and supplies to survivors of a devastating hurricane in Galveston, Texas, in 1900. Not everyone was in support of the Red Cross providing aid during natural disasters, but Barton continued to push for it.

Custer's Last Stand:

Sitting Bull & Crazy Horse's Swift Victory

Many white settlers who came to America from Europe believed the United States belonged to them. They forced the Native Americans who lived there first to give up their lands and relocate further west. Thousands of Native Americans made this difficult journey, which is known as the Trail of Tears.

Native Americans were then forced to live within smaller plots of land in the West, called reservations. Later, when gold was discovered on a reservation in South Dakota, the US Army invaded the region—ignoring the fact that this land now belonged to the tribes.

Sitting Bull and Crazy Horse were leaders of the Sioux on the Great Plains. They always had been against the reservation system because it limited where Native Americans could live and hunt. By spring of 1876, thousands of Native Americans joined Sitting Bull and Crazy Horse by traveling to the Little Bighorn Valley of Montana as a form of revolt.

The government ordered the protesters to return to their reservations, but they didn't listen. When Lieutenant Colonel George Custer and his troops attacked, the Native Americans were ready to defend their land—and they quickly won. This battle is known as "Custer's Last Stand."

60 America's First Roller Coaster: Cheap Thrills in Coney Island

Coney Island, an amusement park in Brooklyn, New York, became the home of the first roller coaster in America in the summer of 1884. The roller coaster was called the Switchback Railway and traveled six miles per hour (10 km/hr). It cost only five cents to ride and was instantly popular, making $600 per day—which would be just under $20,000 a day today!

Its creator, LaMarcus Thompson, got to work thinking of how he could make more—and better—roller coasters. Within three years, Thompson had acquired 30 patents for improvements in roller coasters, like pulling the cars up a hill by a cable, adding emergency stop triggers, and linking several ride vehicles together. By 1888, he had built just under 50 roller coasters in Europe and America.

61 Niagara Falls: State Park Makes a Splash

At the border of Canada and New York is the home to a set of three waterfalls: Horseshoe Falls, American Falls, and Bridal Veil Falls—known together as Niagara Falls.

The amount of water that pours over the falls' ledge is mind-boggling. Every second, tons of water flows over Niagara Falls, producing over four million kilowatts of electricity for the United States and Canada. It's also used for drinking water, boating, fishing, and swimming. Niagara Falls is part of the Great Lakes water system, which is the world's largest surface freshwater system—about 18 percent of the world's supply of fresh water!

In 1885, Niagara Falls was dubbed the "Niagara Reservation," a protected area in the state of New York. At the time, visitors could take horse-drawn carriage rides to admire the falls for $1 per hour. Today, visitors can pay $30 to ride *Maid of the Mist*, a boat that takes you up close. You'll be given a poncho—you're guaranteed to get wet!

62 The Statue of Liberty: From France with Love

Did you know the Statue of Liberty was a gift from France? The monument honors the US centennial, which was the 100-year celebration of the signing of the Declaration of Independence, as well as its friendship with the people of France.

It was sculpted by Frédéric Auguste Bartholdi, who named it "Liberty Enlightening the World." Bartholdi chose the exact site where Lady Liberty would stand—on a small island in the middle of New York Harbor for every ship to see. Gustave Eiffel, the man who built the Eiffel Tower, designed the framework to hold up the enormous statue.

Fun Fact: Lady Liberty is made from copper. When she was unveiled, she was a shiny brown color like a penny. But through a process called oxidation (from rain, wind, and sun), she turned green by 1906.

The statue was built and assembled in Paris, presented to the US minister in France, then disassembled and shipped to the US where it had to be reassembled again upon its arrival. On October 28, 1886, the statue finally was revealed to the cheers of one million New Yorkers who came to see President Grover Cleveland's dedication ceremony.

Lady Liberty stands 305 feet (93 m) tall with a torch raised in her right hand and a book in her left that says, "July 4, 1776." In 1892, the US government opened Ellis Island, a nearby immigration station. Between 1892 and 1954, Lady Liberty welcomed 12 million immigrants on their way to their new life in America.

Thomas Edison's Electric Light Bulb:

Let There Be Light!

Thomas Edison was obsessed with perfecting the light bulb, which had already been invented but burned out in minutes. He was interested in creating a long-burning electric light that could make cities glow all night and was small enough to be used in homes too. At the time, people relied on gas lamps in their homes.

From 1878 to 1880, Edison worked in his laboratory on at least 3,000 different ideas for an incandescent lamp. It used electricity to heat a thin strip of material, called a filament, until it got hot enough to glow, which provided artificial light. It worked fairly well . . . until it burnt out a few hours later.

After years of research, he finally found a filament that lasted even longer. It burned for 13 hours. Edison went on to invent the switches and electric wires that power homes too, which would take decades to install around the country.

Thomas Edison's Kinetoscope:

Moving Pictures Come to Life

Thomas Edison and his assistant William Dickson knew they could make a series of still images look like they were moving. They wanted to create a single camera that could capture those still images very quickly—20 to 30 photographs per second.

Edison and Dickson developed film, a plastic tape that could capture photos, as well as a special camera to go along with it. The new technology allowed the film to stop, capture an image, and move to the next image quickly. They had developed the first video camera! Movies are still filmed this way, 24 frames per second, when they're captured on film.

The duo developed a coin-operated cabinet with a peephole in which customers, one at a time, could watch Dickson's short film in 1891. In 1894, Kinetoscope parlors started popping up around the country. Interested customers could pay five cents, peer into a hole, and watch a 20-to-30-second movie play.

65 Hawaiian Steel Guitar: Joseph Kekuku Makes Music

By 1916, records featuring the Hawaiian steel guitar outsold every other genre of music in America . . . all thanks to Joseph Kekuku. In 1889, when Kekuku was 15 years old in Hawaii, he started experimenting with his Spanish guitar by placing different metal tools, from a bolt to a pocketknife to a metal comb, along the strings. He really liked how it sounded and began sharing his technique. Soon, musicians all over Honolulu began copying Kekuku's style.

Kekuku left Hawaii in 1904 after having perfected his unique way of sliding a polished steel cylinder along the frets (or neck) of his guitar while it sat flat on his lap. He began playing to crowds in San Francisco and soon began touring internationally. At the time, Kekuku was considered the best solo guitarist in the world. Other Hawaiian artists gained popularity around the country too. The Hawaiian steel guitar went on to influence other styles of music and instruments, including the blues slide guitar.

66 Naismith Invents Basketball: He Shoots, He Scores!

In the winter of 1891, a Springfield College graduate student named James Naismith was given a task: to come up with an indoor activity for students to enjoy during the long winters in Massachusetts. The students could play outdoor sports like football and lacrosse in warmer weather, but they were bored with their gym class options during the colder months.

Naismith adapted traits from many other sports to finally come up with a game he called basketball. There was passing (like rugby), a goal (like lacrosse), and a ball (of similar size and shape to soccer). On December 21, Naismith nailed two peach baskets to the balcony in the gymnasium, which was about ten feet (3 m) high. He grabbed a soccer ball and divided the students into two teams. The first basketball game was officially underway.

Ellis Island: Welcome to America!

An immigrant is someone who moves to a new country to live there permanently. From 1850 to 1890, about eight million European immigrants traveled by boat and arrived at the Port of New York looking for a better life in America. It was almost too much for the state of New York to handle. In 1891, the federal government passed the Immigration Act to help the states handle all the new arrivals and they opened a new, larger immigration station on Ellis Island in New York.

Annie Moore, a teenage girl from Ireland, and her two younger brothers were the first to walk through Ellis Island when it opened on January 1, 1892. When immigrants arrived on the island, after a months-long journey across the sea, it took three to five hours to get processed. They would get a health inspection and fill out documents with their name, where they came from, and where they were headed. Any detected sickness meant being sent back home or being forced to stay on the island until they felt better. Interpreters who spoke many different languages helped the immigrants through the process.

As the years went on, 12 million immigrants would pass through—more than all the other American port cities (like San Francisco or New Orleans) combined. Ellis Island's busiest year was 1907 when one million immigrants passed through its doors. At least 40 percent of Americans have at least one ancestor who came through Ellis Island.

68 Tomato Debate: Vegetable or Fruit?

Why would the Supreme Court, the highest court in the US which decides some of the most important cases in history, care whether tomatoes are a fruit or a vegetable? In the 1890s, vegetables had a ten percent import tax, while fruits did not. (A tax is an added fee for every item that is sold.) So, if a tomato was a vegetable, it would cost more! If it was a fruit, it would cost less. No one could decide for sure what it was!

In 1893, Justice Horace Gray decided that even if tomatoes were scientifically a fruit, most Americans considered them a vegetable. Technically, tomatoes develop from a flower and have seeds inside, which make it a fruit, but the reality is that people cook it like a vegetable. The case was settled—legally, tomatoes were classified as a vegetable, so they should be taxed like a vegetable. Do you agree with their decision?

69 The Boston T: Underground Transit

Boston is home to America's first subway tunnel—and it's still in use today! The Tremont Street subway, which was a one-mile (2 km) underground train tunnel on the day it opened in 1897 (and soon stretched to five miles [8 km]), was the first to be built in North America. On that day, thousands of passengers took the three-minute ride joyfully. It may have been short, but it allowed people to travel across the city while avoiding the bad weather and traffic aboveground.

Before the subway train, traveling long distances was tough—most Americans traveled on horseback during the 1700s. By 1856, the city of Boston developed a horse-drawn train car that was pulled along rails. A team of 8,000 horses were pulling passengers around Boston on railcars during this time.

Today, you can experience the historic subway ride by hopping on the Green Line on Boston's Massachusetts Bay Transit Authority. (Locals call it the "T.")

1900–1999

Changing for the Better

70

The Wonderful Wizard of Oz Releases: Off to See the Wizard

Dorothy and her friends, Toto, Tin Man, Scarecrow, and Cowardly Lion, were first introduced to audiences in 1900 when L. Frank Baum's best-selling book, *The Wonderful Wizard of Oz*, hit the shelves. After landing in an unfamiliar world when a tornado hits her hometown, Dorothy and her new friends follow the yellow brick road to meet the Wizard of Oz, who will help her find her way back home to Kansas.

In 1939, a movie version of the book was released starring Judy Garland. *The Wonderful Wizard of Oz* won two Oscars, one for the now-famous song "Over the Rainbow." The movie is the most watched movie in America, according to the Library of Congress.

Fun Fact: The musical, movie, and book *Wicked* is a prequel to *The Wonderful Wizard of Oz*. It tells the origin story of two characters: Glinda the Good Witch and the Wicked Witch of the West.

In the book, Glinda the Good Witch gives Dorothy silver shoes to keep her safe from the Wicked Witch of the West. In the movie, they were a sparkling red color because red shoes stood out better on the yellow brick road. They became known as the "ruby slippers."

Today, there are only four known pairs of the sequined shoes left from the movie. One pair has quite a history. They were stolen from the Judy Garland Museum and were found by the FBI more than ten years later. In 2024, they were auctioned off for $28 million—$32.5 million with taxes and fees. That makes the ruby slippers the most valuable piece of movie history ever.

The Chicago River: The River Runs . . . Backward?

In the late 1800s, Chicago was the fastest-growing city in the world, but it also had the highest death rate in America. The Chicago River flows through its downtown—and those new residents threw their garbage and waste right into the river. Unfortunately, the river flowed into Lake Michigan, which was where the city sourced its drinking water. With waste in the drinking water, diseases spread fast.

The city had a plan: Dig a deep canal that connected the Chicago River to the Des Plaines River, which flowed into the Illinois River and the Mississippi River. Gravity would redirect the wastewater south, which would leave the water clean.

On January 2, 1900, the canal builders blew up the dam that was holding back the Chicago River from flowing south. It worked! Today, this is considered a historic landmark in civil engineering and in public health. The death rate in Chicago finally declined thanks to the cleaner drinking water in Lake Michigan.

Hershey Chocolate: The Real Willy Wonka

You can't hear the word "Hershey" without thinking of "chocolate" today, but entrepreneur Milton Hershey actually became famous for making caramel. A trip to the Chicago World's Fair in 1893 changed everything. He bought German chocolate-making machinery at the fair and quickly began making more than 100 varieties of chocolate in his candy offices in Pennsylvania. In 1900, he shifted his focus to the Hershey Chocolate Company.

Hershey's Milk Chocolate Candy Bar hit the shelves in 1900. An instant hit, the bars were sold for a nickel each. Hershey went on to develop other successes like Hershey's Chocolate Kisses. His factory, in Darry Township, Pennsylvania, became the world's largest chocolate-making business, and a whole city sprung up around it. Today, you can visit that city—now called Hershey, Pennsylvania. It's home to Hershey Park (a theme park with a rollercoaster called Candymonium), the Hotel Hershey (which has chocolate-inspired spa days), and the Hershey Story Museum.

73 Theodore Roosevelt: A President of Many Firsts

The 26th president of the United States, Theodore "Teddy" Roosevelt, had more than one "first." He holds the record for the youngest president at 42 years old. Soon after, he became the first president to invite an African American person, an educator named Booker T. Washington, to dinner at the White House. He also was the first president to have a telephone.

Fun Fact: The "teddy bear" was made in honor of Roosevelt. The president was invited on a hunting trip to shoot a bear, but he refused. The story became famous and stuffed animal shops began selling "Teddy's bears."

In 1902, he became the first president to ride in a car for his presidential duties as he kicked off his tour of New England. He paraded through the streets in Connecticut, waving his hat to the cheering supporters. The car allowed him to see more people in less time. In 1905, he became the first president to board and pilot a submarine—he spent three hours underwater. The next year, he became the first president to leave the country.

He was also the first president to protect wildlife and public land when he created the US Forest Service. It established 150 new national forests and five national parks. Finally, in 1906, he became the first president and the first American to win the Nobel Peace Prize for negotiating peace during a war between Russia and Japan.

Roosevelt was also the first former president to ride in a plane, a plane made by the Wright Brothers. Today, Roosevelt's larger-than-life face is immortalized on South Dakota's Mount Rushmore.

The Wright Brothers: "Flying Machine"

Brothers Wilbur and Orville Wright were the first to invent an airplane! Their "flying machine" was the first powered aircraft that could be piloted.

After starting with kites and gliders, the brothers traveled to North Carolina (for a wide-open space with steady winds) to test out their fourth design attempt in 1903. Orville piloted the first flight, which stayed in the air for 12 seconds. By the time the brothers made their fourth and final flight that day, the plane stayed in the air for 59 seconds—a huge improvement! The 1903 Wright Flyer was refined until their 1905 Flyer became the first practical airplane. It could turn (in a complete circle!) and fly for 39 minutes.

Ice Pop: An Accidental Invention

In 1905, 11-year-old Frank Epperson left a cup of soda with a stirring stick out on the porch. It froze overnight like an icicle. The next day, Epperson pulled it out of the cup and gave it a lick—it was good! He called his invention the "Epsicle" (Epperson + icicle).

Later, Epperson started to sell his cold treats at Neptune Beach, a nearby amusement park in California. Epperson patented the "Epsicle" in 1923. His kids encouraged him to change the name to Pop's 'Sicles, which became the Popsicle® we know today!

St. Louis World's Fair: Introducing Cotton Candy

The St. Louis World's Fair kicked off in 1904. World's Fairs celebrated inventions and technology, and they also included rides and food. Certain foods at the fair, which we now know as very American, became popular after the St. Louis World's Fair.

One Missouri farmer introduced his recipes for nut butter, and festivalgoers got to try peanut butter for the first time. Another vendor ran out of cups for ice cream, so he wrapped up a waffle-like pastry into a cone shape—the first ice cream cone! The fair's biggest hit was "fairy floss," or cotton candy. Crowds were mesmerized by the machine, which spun liquified sugar in a heated bowl 2,200 times per minute.

Lizzie Magie's *Landlord's Game*:

Before *Monopoly*, There Was This!

Did you know that a writer, inventor, and engineer named Lizzie Magie came up with the idea for *Monopoly*? She called it *The Landlord's Game*. In her game, players moved their pieces around a square board where they could buy buildings along the way and charge other players rent.

Magie patented *The Landlord's Game* in 1904, which made her one of the few women in America to hold more than one patent at the time. (Her first was for an improvement to how paper ran through typewriters.) *The Landlord's Game* wasn't super popular, but those who bought it were very big fans—especially college students who were playing it in their economics classes.

In 1933, an unemployed salesman named Charles Darrow was playing a version of *The Landlord's Game*. He slightly redesigned the game by featuring buildings from Atlantic City, New Jersey, and then he claimed he invented the game. He called it *Monopoly*. He filed a copyright, sold it to Parker Brothers, and it became really popular. Darrow went on to become a millionaire.

Magie knew what had happened. A few years later, Parker Brothers ended up buying the rights to *The Landlord's Game* from Magie for $500. Magie never earned millions of dollars like Darrow, and Darrow was known as the creator of *Monopoly* for decades—until the 1970s. Now, Magie is rightfully known as the creator of *Monopoly*'s concept.

Charles Curtis: First Native American US Senator

In 1907, Charles Curtis became the first Native American US senator. He was born in the territory of Kansas, and his heritage included French, Kaw, Osage, and Potawatomi. He learned French and Kansa, which was the language of the Kaw people, and spent his childhood on the Kaw reservation. As a senator, he was heavily involved with the passing of the 19th Amendment, which secured the right for women to vote. Curtis went on to become 31st President Herbert Hoover's vice president, which made him the highest-ranking Native American in the history of the US government.

The Baseball Anthem: Peanuts & Cracker Jacks

There's the national anthem, and then there's "baseball's national anthem." The song, "Take Me Out to the Ball Game," has become the unofficial song of every baseball team around the country, sung during the seventh inning, and one of the top ten songs of the twentieth century. Lyricist Jack Norworth claims he never attended a professional baseball game before writing the 16 lines of the catchy jingle. One of the lyrics, "Buy me some peanuts and Cracker Jacks," helped skyrocket the sales of the crunchy sweet treat. By 1958, Norworth was awarded a lifetime ballpark pass from Major League Baseball.

Angel Island: Ellis Island of the West

While New York's Ellis Island welcomed European immigrants into the United States, Angel Island became the main port of entry for Chinese and Japanese immigrants looking for a new life in the US. Starting in 1910, half a million immigrants came through the island. A majority traveled across the Pacific Ocean from China and other Asian countries, but people also immigrated from Australia, New Zealand, and South America. Asian immigrants had a much different experience than European immigrants on Ellis Island. Upon arrival, the health inspection was followed by an interrogation that could last weeks, months, or years.

81 New Mexico & Arizona: Final Continental States

Up until the 1840s, New Mexico and Arizona were a part of Mexico. It wasn't until the United States won the Mexican–American War in 1848 that the country gained control of the land. New Mexico became a territory, which meant it was owned by the US but wasn't officially a state yet. In 1863, a portion of the New Mexico territory split off and became the Arizona territory.

In 1912, the New Mexico and Arizona Territories became the 47th and 48th states in the country on January 6 and February 14. Arizona was the last state on the continent to join the union. In Arizona, 22 federally recognized tribes live in the state, including the Hopi Tribe, one of the oldest-living cultures, and the Navajo Nation, the largest tribe in the US.

82 Henry Ford's Model T: The Assembly Line Picks Up Speed

By 1908, Henry Ford was already famous for designing the Model T car. It was a simple and inexpensive car made during a time when cars were very expensive and custom-made. But Ford wanted to make the Model T even cheaper.

Initially, a small team of workers in the Detroit, Michigan, factory built each car completely. Ford decided to change that. He divided the car's assembly into 84 separate steps. He trained workers to do one step perfectly. In 1913, he created a moving assembly line. Workers lined up at stations along a conveyor belt. They performed their one task quickly and the unfinished car moved on to the next person. With this new system, a Model T could be built in 90 minutes instead of 12 hours. Ford reduced the price of the car while also making more cars than he ever had before.

Ford also increased his workers' wages and reduced the amount of time they had to work by one hour. Other companies thought he was crazy, but he believed that if he treated his employees well, they'd go on to buy his cars. And they did!

83 **Hollywood:** First Movie Shot in the City of Stars

Hollywood became the center of the movie business in the early 1900s. The first silent movie to be released, *In Old California*, was a 17-minute film that was shot in two days and was one of the first to be shot outdoors. Recording on film was very expensive at the time, so movie studios only filmed in studios (mainly in New York) where the lighting, temperature, and weather could be totally controlled. But Hollywood proved to have warm weather, predictable blue skies, and stunning scenery, which made it a perfect place to film movies. By 1920, Hollywood was the movie capital of the world. Soon going to the movies was America's favorite hobby. Approximately half of the US population went to the movies every week.

Fun Fact: The Hollywood sign originally said "Hollywoodland," but the "land" letters were removed in 1949. Each letter is 45 feet (14 m) tall!

By the 1930s, Hollywood was experiencing its golden age, and the movie industry was one of the largest businesses in America. Movies could now be made with sound and color! Americans enjoyed the latest releases of *Snow White and the Seven Dwarves*, *The Wizard of Oz*, and *Gone with the Wind*. A movie ticket cost 25 to 35 cents at the time and often included a double feature: two movies for the price of one. By the time the 1950s and 1960s rolled around, Hollywood made many musicals with huge productions like *Singin' in the Rain*, *The Sound of Music*, *West Side Story*, and *Mary Poppins*.

84 First Traffic Light: Stop & Go in Cleveland, Ohio

In the early 1900s, the streets of American cities were filled with a mishmash of transportation modes: bicycles, horses, pedestrians, streetcars, and cars. It was a dangerous journey for everyone! Police officers often had to help direct traffic. It wasn't until 1911 that a painted dividing line even appeared on a street.

The world's first electric traffic light was installed in Cleveland, Ohio, in 1914 at a busy intersection. Four pairs of red and green lights (red for "stop" and green for "go") were mounted on corner posts. The lights changed when a traffic officer in a control booth flicked a switch. The design, by James Hoge, was improved upon by African American inventor Garrett Morgan, who received the patent for a three-light setup. Morgan noticed that because there was no "in between" warning between the stop and go lights, collisions still happened. He added a middle red "caution" light that indicated a stop in all directions, an early version of the yellow light.

85 Long-Distance Calls: Coast-to-Coast Conversations

After Alexander Graham Bell invented the telephone in 1876, he never stopped improving upon his technology. In 1915, he was able to make the first transcontinental phone call while sitting in New York City. Bell called his assistant Thomas Watson, who was in San Francisco, and repeated the words he said on his very first phone call to Watson back in 1876: "Mr. Watson, come here. I want to see you." Mr. Watson responded with, "It would take me a week to get to you this time."

By 1920, long-distance phone calls were more common, but only to those who could afford it. Back then, you had to pay for each minute of a long-distance call. Calls that were made to places further away cost more. A ten-minute phone call from Los Angeles to New York cost $26.17 in 1920, which is equivalent to more than $400 today!

The Panama Canal: Moving Mountains (Literally)

Before the Panama Canal existed, the fastest way for boats to travel from the Atlantic Ocean to the Pacific Ocean was by traveling around the southernmost point of South America. The trip took months! It was soon discovered that just a small strip of land separated the two oceans somewhere in Central America—Panama to be exact. If there was a way to clear the land there, people and goods could move much faster from one ocean to the other.

There was just one thing in the way: a nine-mile-long (14 km) mountain range. Clearing the mountain range was very dangerous and took years. Next, a series of locks, devices that can help raise and lower boats, were built. This was needed because the Pacific Ocean sits higher than the Atlantic Ocean. The 12 sets of chambers gradually lift boats above sea level. Crossing the whole path takes eight to ten hours. The Panama Canal became the most expensive construction project in American history at the time.

Piggly Wiggly: First Supermarket

America's first supermarket, Piggly Wiggly, opened in Memphis, Tennessee, in 1916. Created by Clarence Saunders, it was unlike any shopping experience Americans had seen. Before Piggly Wiggly, customers would hand a shopping list to a clerk behind a counter. That clerk would then gather the items for the customer. Saunders noticed that this took a lot of time, and he came up with a better solution: What if customers could shop for themselves?

When the first Piggly Wiggly opened, customers were provided with wooden shopping baskets. For the first time ever, they could reach onto the shelves and grab what they wanted. Saunders made sure each store looked identical, so shoppers could easily find the items they needed regardless of which Piggly Wiggly store they visited. Today, all modern grocery stores use Saunders's "self-serve" shopping concept.

88 Jeanette Rankin: First Woman in Congress

By 1914, 11 states allowed women to vote (plus Illinois, but they only allowed women to vote in the presidential election). When women secured the right to vote in her home state of Montana, suffragist Jeanette Rankin was inspired to run for Congress. On November 7, 1916, Rankin became the first woman elected to US Congress, the first woman in the House of Representatives, and the first woman to hold a federal office in the country. Six other women joined her in the House of Representatives for her second term.

89 Converse Basketball Shoes: Everyone's an All Star

In 1917, a rubber company named Converse released a rubber-soled sneaker with a cotton canvas high top made for the basketball court—it was called the All Star. It wasn't a success until basketball player and coach Chuck Taylor signed with Converse. He became one of the first athletes to sign an endorsement, which is when an athlete partners with a company to help sell a product. Years later, a new and improved (and newly named) Chuck Taylor All Star was released. By 1936, every member of the first US Olympic Basketball team was wearing them. Converse's Chuck Taylor All Star sneakers became the most-purchased sneaker in history.

90 Airmail Begins: Special Delivery from New York to DC

When the US Post Office agreed to deliver mail by plane, there was just one problem: Airplanes were fairly new and not many people knew how to fly them. To begin, the post office hired the Army for its planes and pilots. Six pilots were sent off on May 15, 1918, with hundreds of pounds of mail on their planes, on routes between New York and Washington, DC, with a stop in Philadelphia. By August, the service was deemed a success, and a captain of the Army was chosen to run the official airmail service with its very own special mail planes.

November 11th: World War I Comes to an End

On November 11, 1918, the Great War, known now as World War I, finally ended. On the 11th hour of the 11th day of the 11th month, both sides signed an armistice, which is an agreement to stop fighting. Cheers echoed across America with news of Germany's surrender.

World War I began when Germany invaded Belgium in 1914. In response, one of Belgium's allies (supporters), Britain, declared war on Germany. The war had two sides: the Allies, which were Belgium, Britain, France, Russia, and the United States; and the Central Powers, which were Germany, Austria, Bulgaria, Hungary, and Turkey.

For three years, President Woodrow Wilson tried to keep the US out of the war. But in 1917, the US joined the Allies and declared war against Germany—the first time it had ever joined a war that wasn't fought on its own land. The war was unlike any other—it was the first time tanks, airplanes, submarines, machine guns, flamethrowers, and poison gas were used.

Back home, thousands of American men joined the military while women took up jobs in factories to help make supplies for the war efforts and help replace the men who had left. Women weren't allowed to join the military, but they did volunteer overseas as doctors, nurses, ambulance drivers, and translators.

The following year, President Woodrow Wilson declared November 11 "Armistice Day," as a celebration of the end of the war. Today, November 11 is known as Veterans Day.

The 19th Amendment: Women Vote

When the country was founded in the late 1700s, the rights listed in the Constitution were only granted to white men. Women could not own property, could not vote, and did not technically own any money they earned. By the 1820s, women began protesting and organizing efforts against these limitations—they were known as suffragists.

At first, these suffragists pushed the states to pass laws. And they were successful in convincing 15 states, including California, New York, Arizona, and Kansas. Twelve more states, including Illinois, Rhode Island, Maine, and Wisconsin, let women vote for only the president. But with the passing of the 19th Amendment in 1920, the right for women to vote was now guaranteed for every woman in the country—after 100 years of fighting and 42 years after it was first introduced to Congress. More than eight million women showed up to vote in the election that November.

The 19th Amendment was a huge step forward in the women's rights movement, but the challenging road continued for African American women and women of color who would still find it difficult to vote after its passing.

Madam C. J. Walker: Making a Million

African American entrepreneur Madam C. J. Walker developed her own line of hair products for Black women in the early 1900s. After experiencing hair loss, Walker created a treatment system that became a huge success. It included products like Madam C. J. Walker's Wonderful Hair Grower, Glossine, Vegetable Shampoo, and a wide-tooth hot comb, which is a metal comb that is heated to help straighten hair. Every package included a photo of herself. Walker sold her hair growing and straightening products directly to women, and they quickly grew a following.

Walker trained 40,000 African American sales agents to sell her products directly to customers. In the final year of her life in 1919, sales from her business skyrocketed over $500,000, making her total worth $1 million—the first female ever to become a millionaire. Walker built a life that was far different from the one she was born into. Her parents had both formerly been enslaved. When she passed, she made sure two-thirds of her future business profits would be donated to charitable causes.

Laddie Boy: Celebrity "First Dog"

Laddie Boy wasn't the first "First Dog," but the Airedale terrier was the first presidential dog to become a celebrity and receive regular coverage from the newspapers. As the pet of 29th President Warren G. Harding, Laddie Boy appeared almost daily in *The New York Times* after Harding took office. The terrier went everywhere with the animal-loving president—even to cabinet meetings (where he had his own chair). Laddie Boy even brought the newspaper to Harding each morning.

When Harding sensed that Laddie Boy wasn't getting enough attention in the newspapers, he would write them a letter in the voice of Laddie Boy. After Laddie Boy, "First Dogs" continued to capture Americans' hearts, including Franklin Delano Roosevelt's black Scottie named Fala, who had his own secretary to respond to fan mail.

95 **White Castle:** First Takeout Fast Food

Twenty years before McDonald's, White Castle opened its doors in Wichita, Kansas. The burger shop sold small square-shaped hamburgers, called sliders, for five cents each. They were so easy to eat (and so affordable!) that people bought them in stacks. Within a few years, White Castles were opening across the Midwest.

Founder Billy Ingram wanted every shop to look the same and every burger to taste the same. Each White Castle shop had a grill, a counter, and five stools. The menu had a slider, Coca-Cola, coffee, and apple pie—that was it! A cook (decked out in an all-white uniform, including an apron and a cap) would grill up the burger right in front of the customers and serve it hot. Ingram wanted his customers to see that the burger meat was clean and delicious. Consistency and cleanliness were two ideas Ingram wanted White Castle to represent.

By the end of the 1920s, White Castle had created a hamburger craze—everyone wanted a slider, even in trendy cities like New York. White Castle was so popular that copy-cat restaurants started opening in cities across the country selling small square-shaped sliders and calling themselves names like "White Tower" or "Royal Castle."

Ingram not only created the first fast-food hamburger chain in the US, but he also developed the idea of "takeout" in 1927. His restaurants started selling carry-out bags of burgers with the tagline, "Selling 'em by the Sack."

Bessie Coleman: International Daredevil

When Bessie Coleman passed her flight exam in 1921 at the Fédération Aéronautique Internationale (FAI) in France, she became the first American to be granted the right to fly anywhere in the world—regardless of race or gender. She also became the first African American licensed pilot. When Coleman heard that women were flying in France, she learned French and jumped at the chance.

Coleman's first flight on September 3, 1922, was the first public flight by a Black woman in the US. She soon got a job as a "barnstorming" pilot, which was a popular type of stunt flying in the 1920s. Audiences loved watching her figure eights, loop the loops, and barrel rolls. Sometimes she let her copilot take the controls while she walked out onto the wing or parachuted from the plane.

Coleman stood up for civil rights throughout her career—she refused to perform at one show that was only for white spectators.

Tad Lucas: Yeehaw!

Barbara Ines Barnes Lucas was nicknamed "Tadpole" when she was a baby. She grew up to be "Tad Lucas," the most decorated cowgirl of all time.

Tad entered her first rodeo, a competition where cowboys and cowgirls demonstrate skills like riding horses, in Nebraska at age 14. She won first place then continued to win first place in rodeo competitions around the world. By the time she turned 20 in 1922, she had become a professional cowgirl and had moved to Texas to perform in a wild west show. She traveled through the United States, Mexico, and Europe performing acrobatic tricks atop a horse during the golden age of rodeo. She'd impress audiences by hanging upside down from her saddle, flipping under the horse's belly, climbing up the other side, then standing upright in her stirrups with her arms stretched up to the sky.

The Charleston Dance: The Hottest Move of the 1920s

The 1920s, known as the Roaring Twenties, was an exciting time for the country. For the first time, more Americans lived in cities than on farms, and they had jobs and cars. Most homes had electricity, which brought conveniences like washing machines and vacuum cleaners. Americans finally had more time—and money—to spend on fun stuff. Movies, music, and fashion became favorite pastimes.

A song called "The Charleston" came out in 1923 as part of the Broadway musical *Runnin' Wild*. It had a dance to go along that could be performed alone or with a partner. Either way, dancers moved their legs quickly, bending their knees and turning out their feet, as they stepped forward and backward. Famous dancers like Josephine Baker added their own style to the dance and soon the country couldn't get enough of the new dance craze. Charleston competitions were held in theaters and people were asked, "Can you do the Charleston?"

The Grand Ole Opry: Live Country Music

Started in 1925, the Grand Ole Opry is a live country music show that is broadcast over the radio in Nashville, Tennessee—and it's still going! For the first time, audiences could listen to a live musical variety show. It was basically a concert on the radio. Southern audiences loved the Saturday night show. Local crowds clogged the hallways of the fifth-floor recording studio to watch the musicians in person. Eventually, the show moved to a nearby theater so the Grand Ole Opry could play to live audiences at the same time.

The Opry became known as the "show that made country music famous." Country music stars like Dolly Parton and Johnny Cash have performed at the Opry. Today, you can get tickets to a live show where country music's biggest and up-and-coming artists perform at the 4,372-seat Opry House theater.

Balto the Husky: Hero in Nome, Alaska

During the winter of 1925, a deadly infection was spreading fast in a town in Alaska, just below the Arctic Circle. Twenty children were sick, and it would continue to spread to other people without life-saving medicine. However, it was so cold that planes couldn't fly there. The only way to get this medicine was to organize multiple dog sled teams to make the harrowing journey to the nearest train station, which was far away.

Fun Fact: An animated movie called *Balto* came out in 1995. In this version, Balto befriends a goose named Boris and two polar bears who run with him.

The governor organized twenty volunteers along the route who gathered up their best Siberian huskies. One volunteer, Gunna Kaasen, chose a young newbie: three-year-old Balto. A 20-pound (9 kg) package of medicine arrived at the train station on January 27. The first dog sled team grabbed it, rode for hours, then passed it onto the next team.

More dog sled teams ran an average of 30 miles (48 km) in freezing temperatures over the course of five days until they finally reached the last team: Kaasen and Balto. Despite Balto's little experience, he swiftly carried the medicine more than 50 miles (80 km) through a blizzard and into Nome, mostly using his sense of smell to guide them along the correct path. Three weeks later, the disease had stopped spreading and the residents of Nome were deemed safe—all thanks to the husky dogs' brave efforts.

Balto's legacy still lives on: Every March, sled dog teams compete in the Iditarod Trail Sled Dog Race following the same route.

101 The Father of Black History: A Momentous Month

The United States has been celebrating Black History Month for over 100 years thanks to educator Dr. Carter G. Woodson, who is known as the "father of Black history."

In 1915, Dr. Woodson was inspired to celebrate Black history and the achievements of Black people, which he felt was missing from American history lessons. (Black history was literally missing from history textbooks in school classrooms!) He felt that history could inspire people to achieve even more in the future. Dr. Woodson created an organization whose main goal was to study Black history. The next year, it published the first scholarly journal that featured research about Black culture.

Dr. Woodson declared Negro History Week in February of 1926. He chose February because it was the month both Abraham Lincoln and Frederick Douglass were born, two leaders and activists for African American rights. The proclamation inspired schools and communities around the country to bring attention to Black history for one week.

Students at Kent State University proposed turning Negro History Week into Black History Month, and they celebrated it for the first time in February of 1970. The nation soon followed in February of 1976. Today, we continue to celebrate Black history throughout the month of February by learning about the important achievements of African Americans and how they've shaped American history.

Harlem Globetrotters: World's Best Team

The Harlem Globetrotters started in Chicago as a serious basketball team. At the time, basketball was segregated, which means there were separate teams for white players and Black players. The all-Black Globetrotters had their first game in January of 1927 and played wherever they could.

In 1948 and again in 1949, the Globetrotters beat the World Champion all-white NBA team, the Minneapolis Lakers, in an exhibition game—making the Globetrotters the world's best basketball team and helping to bring attention to African American players. Globetrotter Nathaniel "Sweetwater" Clifton became the first African American player to sign with the NBA when he joined the New York Knicks in 1950. This marked the first time the NBA was officially integrated, which meant both white and Black players could play on the same team.

Today, the Harlem Globetrotters are an exhibition team, which means they play for fun. They are known for their amazing performances, which mix incredible basketball tricks, comedy, and fun. They've traveled to 124 countries on six continents.

More S'mores!: Girl Scouts Invent a Camping Treat

In 1927, a Girl Scouts manual called "Tramping and Trailing with the Girl Scouts" included recipes that were great for an overnight hiking trip. One recipe for a sweet treat was called "Some More," as in "I want some more!" It instructed readers to "toast two marshmallows over the coals to a crisp gooey state," then put them inside a sandwich made from a graham cracker and a chocolate bar. The recipe finished with, "Though it tastes like 'some more,' one is really enough." It is believed the recipe may have been created at a Girl Scouts camp in Briarcliff Manor, New York. The Girl Scouts went on to create an official "S'more" cookie, which they sold during their annual cookie sales.

104 Babe Ruth: Yankees Player Runs the Bases

The 1927 New York Yankees are considered the greatest baseball team of all time, and on their team was the greatest player of his time. When player Babe Ruth hit his 60th home run on September 30, 1927, he set a home run record that stuck for the next 34 years.

Ruth started his career with the Boston Red Sox. His new teammates gave him the nickname, "Babe," because he was so young—just 19 years old. He'd go on to have other nicknames, including the "Bambino" and the "Sultan of Swat." He played with the team for five years, and they won three World Series during this time. But at the end of the season, they sold off Ruth to the New York Yankees for $100,000. Fans were shocked.

During the 15 years Ruth played for the New York Yankees, the team won four World Series. Meanwhile, the Boston Red Sox winning streak had come to an end—in fact, the team did not win another World Series until 2004 when the "Curse of the Bambino" was finally broken. In 1935, Ruth hit his 714th and final home run—a record that was not beaten until 1974 by the Atlanta Brave player, Hank Aaron.

Bread-Slicing Machine:
The Best Thing Since . . . Well, Sliced Bread!

Have you heard the phrase, "It's the best thing since sliced bread"? Well, there was a time when slicing bread wasn't popular. In 1928, Otto Frederick Rohwedder developed the automatic bread-slicing machine for a bakery in Missouri. Bakeries around the country could quickly slice bread in neat and even pieces at the perfect width—just under half an inch (1 cm). But shoppers weren't so sure. Some bakers thought it was just a fad. Within a couple years, Americans came to love it—until World War II when bread-slicing machines were banned to save steel. Suddenly, Americans had to find serrated bread knives for the first time in decades and risked nicking their fingers with each slice. The ban only lasted two months, and Americans finally got their sliced bread back.

Disney's "Steamboat Willie": Meet Mickey Mouse!

In November of 1928, Mickey Mouse (and Minnie!) made their debut in a cartoon called "Steamboat Willie." The black-and-white short was also the first cartoon to be synchronized with sound. Lots of silly sound effects matched up with the animation. When Mickey pulled the horn, it tooted. When the cow opened its mouth, it mooed. When Minnie ran, her heels clacked.

"Steamboat Willie" debuted in New York City as a cartoon that played before longer films—and it was an instant hit. Walt Disney and his lead animator Ub Iwerks got to work creating more cartoons featuring the now-famous mouse, and Disney provided the voice of Mickey Mouse for at least 100 shorts. Today, Mickey Mouse is considered to be the most recognized symbol in the world—even more than Santa Claus.

Fun Fact: Disney originally wanted to call his new mouse character Mortimer. His wife, Lillian, suggested the name "Mickey" instead.

Empire State Building:
World's Tallest Building Rises in NYC

New York City's Empire State Building is the most photographed building in the world. When construction started in 1930, it was designed to be the world's first building over 100 stories. It was built in a record-setting one year and 45 days by 3,000 workers. The Empire State Building opened May 1, 1931, as the world's tallest building at 102 stories and 1,250 feet (381 m). Its Art Deco style perfectly showcased the glamorous 1920s.

Tourists loved heading to the 86th floor for the tearoom and soda fountain and to the 102nd floor for the observation deck. For ten cents, visitors could peer through a telescope—and within six months of opening, the building had collected more than $3,000 in coins (that's almost $63,000 today!). Two years later, the movie *King Kong* (page 80) was released in theaters, which features the giant gorilla climbing to the top of the now-famous building.

The American Society of Civil Engineers named the Empire State Building one of the seven greatest American engineering achievements. Since 1976, the lights of the iconic Empire State Building change colors for important occasions and holidays, like pink for Valentine's Day.

Duke Ellington: Composing the Anthem of Swing

Duke Ellington is one of the greatest jazz composers of all time and his performances are some of the most popular from the big band era. He toured the world as a band leader, piano player, and composer, and led his jazz orchestra for over 50 years.

During the 1930s and 1940s, swing music was a nationwide craze. The upbeat jazz tunes inspired people to get up and dance. When Ellington released his instant hit, "It Don't Mean a Thing (If It Ain't Got That Swing)," it stayed on the Billboard charts for six weeks in 1932.

Before his hit song, Ellington was known for playing at the Cotton Club with his band in the 1920s. It was a club in Harlem for white people only. Ellington and his band had to enter through the back door because they were Black. Ellington used his music, which includes more than 2,000 songs, to unite people. By 1961, Ellington refused to play for segregated audiences.

Hattie Wyatt Caraway: First Elected Female Senator

In 1932, Hattie Wyatt Caraway became the first woman elected to the US Senate. After her husband, Arkansas Senator Thaddeus Caraway, suddenly died, she won a special election to fill the rest of her husband's term. She beat out two male opponents.

No one thought she'd run for reelection in 1932 when her term came to an end, but she did. Six men ran against her, but she won in a landslide. Caraway became a quiet advocate for women's rights and had to fight for her place in an all-male work environment.

She ran for reelection in 1938 when one of her male opponents had the slogan, "Arkansas Needs Another Man in the Senate." She beat him too, and she served as a Senator until 1945. On her last day of service, her all-male peers gave her a standing ovation.

110 Amelia Earhart: Flying Solo

Five years after Charles Lindbergh became the first person to fly solo across the Atlantic Ocean, Amelia Earhart became the first pilot to repeat the journey—and the first woman to do so. She left from Newfoundland, Canada, and landed in Londonderry, Northern Ireland, on May 20, 1932.

Earhart set many other records: She became the first woman to fly solo above 14,000 feet (4 km). She was the first woman to make a flight across the Atlantic Ocean as a passenger. In 1932, after piloting her historic transatlantic flight, she became the first woman to fly solo across the US on her flight from Los Angeles to New Jersey. A few years later, she became the first person (of any gender) to fly solo from Hawaii to the US mainland. Earhart's many feats pushed women in aviation forward.

Always reaching for the next record, Earhart left on a journey to fly around the globe in 1937. It was her second attempt to become the first pilot to circle the globe. She and her flight navigator Fred Noonan left from California, and over the next month, they stopped to fuel up in Florida, South America, Africa, India, and southeast Asia. When they arrived in New Guinea a month later, they had flown 22,000 miles (35,405 km) and had only 7,000 more miles (11,265 km) to go. Earhart's plane disappeared somewhere over the Pacific Ocean soon after. Her disappearance continues to be one of the greatest unsolved mysteries of the twentieth century.

111 **King Kong:** Gorilla Takes NYC & Hollywood

When *King Kong* opened in theaters on March 2, 1933, audiences went "ape" for it. In its first four days, it earned $90,000 (just over $2 million today). The movie features an oversized gorilla and a famous scene where Kong climbs on top of the Empire State Building holding the female lead character, Ann, while planes swarm around him.

The movie featured practical effects like stop-motion animation and the use of miniatures, including an 18-inch-tall (46 cm) gorilla puppet and a small-scale model of the Empire State Building, to make it appear that a giant monster was taking over New York City. Although the special effects were not very believable, audiences loved it. An era of "monster movies" followed.

112 **Eleanor Roosevelt:** Making Waves as the First Lady

First Lady Eleanor Roosevelt, wife of 32nd President Franklin Delano Roosevelt (page 87), turned heads when she held her own press conferences as a First Lady—and only invited female reporters. At the time, White House press conferences could only be attended by men. Plus, no First Lady had ever held a press conference before.

On March 6, 1933, she began a series of 348 women's-only press conferences during her record-setting 12 years as a First Lady. At the press conferences, Eleanor shared her schedule as a First Lady but also helped promote the work of female leaders. She was the first First Lady to speak openly with the press, an act that encouraged women to stay informed and get politically involved.

Eleanor often toured the country on the president's behalf because he was in a wheelchair due to polio, and what she observed fueled her to become more outspoken. She went on to fight for civil rights, women's rights, and human rights, and she traveled overseas to visit soldiers during wartime.

113 **Hoover Dam:** An Engineering Marvel

When the Hoover Dam was completed in 1935, the 60-story-tall structure was the largest dam in the world. Named one of America's seven modern wonders of civil engineering, the Hoover Dam helped tame the Colorado River and provide water and power to the American Southwest. It helped cities like Los Angeles, Las Vegas, and Phoenix grow into the cities they are today.

Located on the Arizona–Nevada border in a desert about 30 miles (48 km) outside of Las Vegas, the dam was difficult to build. It took five years and involved blasting canyon walls, digging tunnels, and working in extreme heat. Five hundred houses were built in Boulder City, Nevada, to house the dam workers and their families—an entire new city for one tough project.

114 **Golden Gate Bridge:** Photogenic in San Francisco

The iconic two-mile-long (3 km) Golden Gate Bridge connects San Francisco with Marin County, California. It stretches north across the Golden Gate, which is a narrow opening where the San Francisco Bay meets the Pacific Ocean.

It was the first time a bridge support was built in the middle of the ocean—and divers had to swim 90 feet (27 m) below the surface to blast away rock. During construction, a safety net was hung from one end of the bridge to the other. It helped save the lives of 19 men. The Golden Gate Bridge finally opened after four long years of construction on April 19, 1937. The following day was declared a "Pedestrian Day," and 200,000 Californians lined up to cross the bridge that day.

The Golden Gate Bridge is believed to be the most photographed bridge in the world, and it joined the list of America's seven modern wonders of civil engineering in 1994.

115

Snow White and the Seven Dwarfs:

First Animated Feature

When Walt Disney decided to release a feature-length film that was entirely animated, critics thought it was a horrible idea. They called it, "Disney's Folly." But when *Snow White and the Seven Dwarfs* premiered in Los Angeles on December 21, 1937, audiences were captivated. They cried when the prince awoke Snow White from her slumber—even though it was just a cartoon—proving that animation could be beautiful, emotional, and exciting for grown-ups too. The film received a standing ovation from the celebrity-filled audience. (Actors Charlie Chaplin, Judy Garland, and Shirley Temple were there!)

Critics agreed: *Snow White* was unlike anything they had ever seen before—and they were right! It was the first animated feature in America. It took three long years to make with millions of hand-painted and hand-drawn images. For the movie, Disney created an innovation called the multiplane camera, which could move through layers of painted backgrounds to help make the animation look more detailed and give it literal depth.

The movie made the studio a lot of money and allowed Disney to build a new studio in California. At the Academy Awards in 1939, Disney was given a special award for *Snow White and the Seven Dwarfs*. It featured one large Oscar with seven smaller ones beside it. Today, the Academy Awards have a special category for Animated Films, and three Disney and Pixar movies have been nominated for Best Picture: *Beauty and the Beast, Up,* and *Toy Story 3*.

116

Chocolate Chip Cookie: Ruth Wakefield's Sweet Invention

Ruth Wakefield ran the Toll House Inn and loved serving her customers sweet treats, like their best-selling thin butterscotch nut cookie. Wakefield started brainstorming what else she could do with cookie dough to satisfy sweet tooths. She grabbed a Nestlé chocolate bar and chopped the bar into pea-size chunks. She added them to the dough and baked the cookie—and the chunks of chocolate didn't melt. Wakefield served them to her customers, and they soon became known as Toll House Cookies. She printed the recipe for "Chocolate Crunch Cookies" in a 1938 cookbook called *Ruth Wakefield's Tried and True Recipes*. The next year, she sold the rights to the recipe to Nestlé, and you can still find it printed on each package of semisweet chocolate morsels today.

117

Televised Baseball: Take Me Out . . . to the Living Room

On May 17, 1939, people who had never seen a baseball game finally got the chance to see one on TV. It was the first time a baseball game aired on television. The game, between the universities Princeton and Columbia, was captured by a single camera which was set up 50 feet (15 m) from home plate. That meant viewers at home had a pretty bad view of the game, but it was still exciting! Most baseball fans were used to listening on the radio. The new technology of TV had potential, but most Americans didn't have one—yet.

118

Mount Rushmore: Four Faces of American Democracy

In South Dakota's Black Hills, visitors can find the 60-foot-high (18 m) faces of four US Presidents carved into stone: George Washington, Thomas Jefferson, Abraham Lincoln, and Theodore Roosevelt. It took more than ten years to make one of the world's largest sculptures. Almost half a million tons of rock were blasted away from the almost 6,000-foot (2 km) granite mountain.

Each head received a dedication ceremony as it was finished, and the completed Mount Rushmore finally opened on October 31, 1941.

119 **Rosie the Riveter:** "We Can Do It!"

Once the United States joined World War II in December of 1941, many men enlisted in the military to fight overseas. That left many jobs open in the US with no one to fill them. At the time, women did not often work outside of the home. Rosie the Riveter was a fictional character created to encourage women to take on a factory job during World War II—it was patriotic, after all! By 1945, almost one out of every four married women worked outside the home.

Rosie the Riveter's image first appeared with the tagline, "We Can Do It!" on a recruitment poster by illustrator J. Howard Miller. She wore an iconic red and white polka-dot scarf tied around her head. The next year, a song was released called "Rosie the Riveter," which finally gave a name to the iconic poster image.

During World War II, women also helped in the military both at home and abroad. By 1945, there were more than 100,000 Women's Army Corp (page 85) members and 6,000 female officers working important noncombat jobs, like drivers, mechanics, and typists. Women took to the skies too. More than 1,000 women joined the Women's Airforce Service Pilots (WASP), which were women who had already obtained their pilot's licenses. They transported cargo and more.

After World War II, the workplace had been changed forever—women were now a part of the picture.

120 Wonder Woman: Truth, Justice & Girl Power

American kids met Superman in 1938, Batman a year later, and Captain America in 1941. They finally met Wonder Woman in 1942. She was featured on the cover of *Sensation Comics* for its debut issue in January of that year.

Wonder Woman is the alter ego of Princess Diana of Themyscira. Diana was a trained Amazon warrior and lived on the all-female Paradise Island. Her iconic items included a "Lasso of Truth," an invisible jet, and thick gold cuff bracelets for protection. Many of her early comics featured Wonder Woman supporting US soldiers during World War II. Wonder Woman's early comics included sidebars featuring "Wonder Women of History," which were real-life stories of famous career women in history.

The comics were turned into a popular film and TV show in the 1970s, starring Lynda Carter, and then another film in 2017, starring Gal Gadot.

121 The Women's Army Auxiliary Corp: Women Join the Army

Before World War II, women in the military could only serve as Army or Navy nurses. First Lady Eleanor Roosevelt and Massachusetts Representative Edith Nourse Rogers helped push for a women's service branch in the Army. In May of 1942, President Franklin Delano Roosevelt signed the act that established the Women's Auxiliary Army Corp. It soon became an official part of the Army, instead of a service that supported them, and changed its name to the Women's Army Corp (WAC).

Although thousands of women had assisted during the Revolutionary War, Civil War, and World War I, this was the first time women were recognized as members of the Army. That meant they would finally get equal pay, rank, and benefits as the men.

World War II: A War to End All Wars

In 1941, war was at America's doorstep but had been raging in Europe for years.

A dangerous man named Adolf Hitler and the Nazi Party were leading Germany. Hitler believed that Germany should take over Europe, so he began invading nearby countries, including Poland. He focused on capturing and killing Jewish people, which is now known as the Holocaust. Great Britain and France, in support of Poland, declared war on Germany. They became known as the Allies. Germany joined forces with Italy and Japan, and they became known as the Axis powers. World War II had begun.

Fun Fact: *The Diary of a Young Girl* is a real-life diary written by Anne Frank, a Jewish child hiding in Amsterdam during World War II. It's sold tens of millions of copies worldwide and is one of the most-read accounts of the Holocaust.

In December of 1941, the Japanese bombed Pearl Harbor, a military base in Honolulu, Hawaii. The US declared war on Japan and then Germany. On June 6, 1944 (now known as D-Day), the Allies successfully landed on the beaches of Normandy, France, and began freeing cities that Nazi Germany had taken over across Europe. On May 8, 1945, Germany surrendered.

But the United States was still fighting with Japan. At home, the US government imprisoned Japanese Americans and Japanese immigrants. Then President Harry Truman authorized the first-ever use of an atomic bomb, which the US dropped on the Japanese cities of Hiroshima and Nagasaki in August of 1945, killing more than 120,000 people. Japan surrendered on September 2, 1945.

World War II was the biggest and deadliest war in history, with 60 to 80 million lives lost— including the lives of six million Jewish people and 400,000 Americans. In January of 1942, President Franklin Delano Roosevelt created what is now known as the United Nations. The organization gathered 26 nations who were interested in keeping international peace.

123 **Four–Term President:** Franklin Delano Roosevelt

Franklin Delano Roosevelt became the 32nd president in November of 1932—and he is the only president to serve four terms (or three terms!). America's first president, George Washington, had set a precedent to only serve two terms. Roosevelt broke that tradition when he ran for a third term in the 1940 election during World War II.

Roosevelt was elected for the fourth time in November of 1944, after the United States had entered the war. Today, the 22nd Amendment, passed just two years after Roosevelt's death in 1945, limits the president to two terms.

Fun Fact: Roosevelt is one of the first presidents to directly and routinely communicate with the American people. His "fireside chats" on the radio eventually moved to the TV.

124 **Jackie Robinson:** First African American MLB Player

Jackie Robinson is a man of firsts. In college, Robinson became the University of California–Los Angeles's first four-sport student athlete when he played football, basketball, baseball, and track and field. After serving in the US Army during World War II, he joined the segregated Negro Leagues's baseball league as a shortstop in Kansas.

In 1945, Robinson was invited to join the all-white Brooklyn Dodgers' practice league, the Montreal Royals, making him the first African American to play on a Major League Baseball team. On April 15, 1947, he was promoted to first baseman with the Brooklyn Dodgers, wearing jersey No. 42.

Robinson wasn't treated like an equal to his teammates, but that year, Robinson took home the first-ever Rookie of the Year Award. In 1949, he won the Most Valuable Player Award. He became a World Series Champion in 1955. In 1962, Robinson became the first African American to be inducted in the Baseball Hall of Fame.

125 Polaroid Camera: An Instant Success!

The instant Polaroid camera first sold at a department store in Boston for $89.75—and it sold out within minutes. The camera was invented by chemist Edwin H. Land. After snapping a photo, a piece of film would instantly pop out of the camera, and within 60 seconds, the developed image would appear on the film.

Land's three-year-old daughter inspired him because she wanted to see the photo *now*. Back then, you couldn't see the photos until they were developed by a lab and printed onto glossy paper, which could take days. From days to seconds, Polaroid was an instant success.

126 45 Minutes of Music: Long-Playing Vinyl Record

For almost 100 years, people listened to music on records. The Columbia LP Microgroove was a 12-inch (30 cm) circular disc that played music for 45 minutes. It was called an "LP" for short, which stood for "long-playing." Before the LP, 12-inch records could only play eight minutes worth of music.

Records were played on a record player where an arm with a needle started at the edge of the record as it spun, reading the grooves (an imprint of sound waves) and turning them into sound. There was no way to fast-forward or rewind. After 23 minutes, you'd flip over the disc and play the other side.

127 Mr. Potato Head: Play with Your Food

When Mr. Potato Head was first created, inventor George Lerner was trying to come up with a toy that could make vegetables more fun, so he designed plastic body parts that could stick into a real potato. It was basically a potato decorating kit!

Lerner's plastic parts were first distributed as prizes in cereal boxes, but then Hasbro, a toy company, noticed his fun idea and bought the rights. On April 30, 1952, they released a Mr. Potato Head commercial. Later, kids met Mrs. Potato Head and their children, Yam and Spud. It wasn't until 1962 that Hasbro created a plastic potato body, so kids would stop playing with moldy potatoes!

128 The Dover Sun House: First Solar-Powered Home

No one had ever lived in a house that was heated by the sun until the Dover Sun House, the first fully solar-powered home. The project was created by engineer and biophysicist, Dr. Mária Telkes, who became known as the "Sun Queen." She invented more than 20 methods to capture energy from the sun to heat homes and even operate a portable oven at 350 degrees Fahrenheit (177°C). The house served as a successful example for the solar energy field that would continue for many years to come.

129 Brown v. Board: Separate Isn't Equal

After the Civil War, many people believed that it was okay to segregate, or separate, people in physical spaces. For example, there would be a bathroom for white people and a different one for Black people. As long as it was "equal" in quality, it was deemed okay. "Separate but equal" became a common phrase back then.

In the 1950s, the National Association for the Advancement of Colored People (NAACP) gathered court cases across the country about segregation in schools and presented it as one case: *Brown v. Board of Education* in 1954. They proved separate was not always equal. Black students often had to travel farther away from their neighborhood to Black schools, and they didn't have access to school buses, nice buildings, or books. The Supreme Court agreed to legally end segregation in public schools in the US.

Four years later in 1960, six-year-old Ruby Bridges faced racism as the first Black student to attend a previously all-white school in New Orleans. Bridges had to be guarded when she entered the school, and 500 students were taken out of school that day.

Bridges bravely continued to go to school and was often taught alone. By second grade, Bridges's class was integrated and more Black students attended.

130 **Disneyland's Opening Day:** Millions Tune In on TV

In the 1950s, Walt Disney wanted to build an amusement park near Los Angeles, but the city of Burbank didn't like his idea. He found a bigger and better location—Anaheim, California—and a fast-paced year-long construction schedule began in 1954.

Disney helped fund the theme park by filming its progress and sharing updates throughout the year on a weekly television show. By the time Disneyland opened on July 17, 1955, the whole nation was excited to see Frontierland, Tomorrowland, Adventureland, Fantasyland, and Main Street, U.S.A.

Opening day aired on live TV in an ABC broadcast titled "Dateline: Disneyland." It did not go as planned—15,000 fake tickets had been created, so the park overflowed with visitors. The park ran out of food and water, and ladies' high heels got stuck in the freshly poured asphalt, but Americans had fallen in love with the new theme park.

131 **Route 66:** Road Trips Made Fun—and Fast!

In 1926, the first highway system in the US opened, which meant roads were finally getting paved and connected to make long-distance travel easier and quicker. In 1938, Route 66 became the first completely paved highway in the country. Sometimes called the "Mother Road," Route 66 stretches from Illinois to California, and it winds through eight states.

After World War II, car ownership boomed. Families had access to cars and vacation time, and Route 66 became their path out west to hot spots like the Santa Monica Pier, the Grand Canyon, and Disneyland. Tourists drove through small towns along the way, eating at diners, staying at motels, shopping at gift shops, and admiring roadside attractions, like the very first McDonald's in California.

132 **Rosa Parks:** A Seat for Civil Rights

When civil rights activist Rosa Parks walked onto a city bus on December 1, 1955, she took a seat in the back. In Montgomery, Alabama, Black passengers were only allowed to sit in the back of buses. When the white section was filled up front, the driver asked her and three other Black passengers to stand up so white passengers could take their seats in the first row of the Black section—but she wouldn't do it.

The 42-year-old Parks was jailed for not giving up her seat. Her brave actions set off a movement called the Montgomery Bus Boycott, which was led by Martin Luther King, Jr. Parks's trial was set days later, and Black residents of Montgomery decided to boycott the bus to support her.

Parks was found guilty of violating segregation laws and fined $14. The bus boycott continued all year. Parks lost her job as a seamstress at the department store, but she stayed focused on the movement. On November 13, 1956, bus segregation was ruled unconstitutional. The Montgomery Bus Boycott finally ended one year later on December 20.

Elvis Presley: "Hound Dog" Drops Jaws

Elvis Presley was known as the King of Rock 'n' Roll, and his performance on the *Milton Berle Show* is what earned him the crown.

In June of 1956, Presley did something he'd never done on TV before as 40 million people watched live. He set aside his acoustic guitar, which allowed him to dance while he sang. The 21-year-old was already famous, but that night, his dance moves went down in history.

Presley bent his knees, shook his hips, and stood on his toes while he hung onto the microphone and sang, "You ain't nothing but a hound dog" from his new song, "Hound Dog." The performance made him an international superstar.

In the 1950s, his dance moves caused a lot of fuss, but they would be considered pretty tame today. For Elvis's next TV appearance, host Ed Sullivan asked him to sing "Hound Dog" to a Basset hound wearing a top hat. It took the attention away from his dancing.

Presley went on to sell over one billion records—and star in 33 successful films during the 1950s and 1960s, including *Blue Hawaii*. His many hits, "Heartbreak Hotel," "Jailhouse Rock," "Blue Suede Shoes," and "Can't Help Falling in Love," are still favorites today. You can visit Graceland, his home-turned-museum, in Memphis, Tennessee, today.

134 Dalip Singh Saund: A Congressman Like No Other

Dalip Singh Saund made history in 1956 when he won the election for US Representative for the state of California. He became the first Asian American, Indian American, Sikh American, and Indian immigrant to serve in Congress.

Saund was born in Punjab, India, in 1899, and moved to the US for college. He earned a PhD in mathematics, but Saund ended up working as a lettuce farmer for 20 years. In 1946, Congress passed a bill allowing Indian immigrants the chance to become American citizens, and he finally became one in 1949.

When he ran for Congress, Saund ended up winning—and won two more reelections after that. During his time in the House of Representatives, he fought on behalf of California farmers and the Civil Rights Movement and took a goodwill trip to India for the US State Department.

135 The Little Rock Nine: Civil Rights in the Classroom

Daisy Bates ran *The Arkansas Weekly*, one of the only African American newspapers that exclusively covered the civil rights movement. When the Supreme Court ruled that segregated schools were unconstitutional in 1954, Bates helped African American students enroll at all-white schools in Arkansas, but some of these schools would not let Black students enroll even years later.

In September of 1957, Bates personally recruited nine Black students who would integrate into the all-white Central High School in Little Rock. She—and the students she chose—knew it wouldn't be easy. When they showed up on September 4, they were greeted by hostile protests, threats from the Arkansas governor, and the National Guard, which had been sent to keep them out. The Little Rock Nine never made it inside the school that day, but they showed up again on September 29. This time, President Dwight D. Eisenhower sent US Army troops to escort the five boys and four girls into the high school. They made it inside, and the school was finally integrated.

136 **NASA:** America Travels to Space

Americans put a man on the moon, robots on Mars, and satellites (that help us forecast weather and navigate the globe) into space—all thanks to NASA.

In 1957, the Soviet Union sent *Sputnik I*, the world's first satellite, into orbit. The basketball-sized satellite orbited Earth for just 98 minutes. Americans always thought the United States would be first in the so-called "space race." The following month, the Soviet Union launched *Sputnik II*, and this time a dog named Laika was on board. The US had to act fast—and finally sent its own satellite to space in January of 1958.

As the US became serious about its space program, the National Aeronautics and Space Administration (NASA) officially opened later that year. The race was on to send the first person to space. In 1961, the US sent NASA astronaut Alan Shepard into space—but it was one month after Yuri Gagarin from the Soviet Union became the first person in space. The US would have to settle for second—but not for long!

In 1969, Neil Armstrong and Buzz Aldrin became the first humans to walk on the moon. America had finally pulled ahead in the space race. From then on, NASA continued to rise to the top. In 1976, the *Viking I* landed on Mars. Sally Ride (page 120) became the first American woman in space (and soon after became the first American woman to go to space twice!) while Bluford (pictured) became the first African American in space.

137 Alaska & Hawaii: The Final 50

Seven months after Alaska became the 49th state in January of 1959, Hawaii joined the union as the 50th state on August 21, 1959. Both states had been US territories for decades before joining the union.

The United States purchased Alaska from Russia in 1867. Americans knew it was rich in resources like gold, petroleum, and seafood. Hawaii's path to statehood was more complex. It started as an independent country, but in 1893, a group of American sugar planters overthrew the Hawaiian monarch, Queen Lili'uokalani. In 1898, Hawaii became a US territory and a naval base before it officially became a US state.

138 Air Travel: Americans Fly High

Americans who wanted to travel by sea across the Atlantic Ocean could expect it to take four or five days each way. So when the first modern passenger plane to fly from North America to Europe took to the skies in 1945, people were excited to travel farther and faster. It was a slow propeller plane, so it had to stop for fuel twice before landing. Travel could take almost a full day—still faster than boat travel! Once jets became the norm, air travel became popular. A flight from New York City to London could now take seven hours on a jet instead of 15 hours on a propeller plane.

139 *The Sound of Music*: A New Broadway Hit

The Sound of Music premiered on Broadway on November 16, 1959, and became an overnight hit. Songs like "Do-Re-Mi" and "My Favorite Things" became pop culture favorites. The musical tells the story of Maria, a governess for seven children, who ends up marrying their father. The family escapes Austria as World War II erupts.

The Sound of Music was created by Richard Rodgers and Oscar Hammerstein, a famous musical team that were also known for *Oklahoma!*

Fun Fact: In 1965, *The Sound of Music* was released in theaters and starred Julie Andrews. It became the most popular movie musical ever made.

140 Meet Barbie: Ruth Handler Unveils Her New Doll

When Barbie was introduced at the New York Toy Fair in 1959, she wore a black-and-white-striped swimsuit, sunglasses, and a long ponytail. She sold for $3 and was unlike any other doll at the time. Barbie was an adult woman—all other dolls were baby dolls. Some people didn't think kids would like her, but they were so wrong. Mattel sold 300,000 Barbie dolls that year.

Fun Fact: An original Barbie was sold in an auction for $27,450 in 2006. But that's not the most expensive Barbie sold. The glamorous Stefano Canturi Barbie sold for $302,500 in 2010—it featured a real diamond necklace and raised money for breast cancer research.

Barbie was invented by Ruth Handler, who named the doll after her teenage daughter Barbara. After watching her daughter play with paper dolls, she realized girls needed a lifelike adult doll they could play with. It could help teach girls that they could grow up to be anything. Handler created an extensive wardrobe of outfits for Barbie, who has had many different careers over the decades, including astronaut, CEO, and president.

Handler cofounded Mattel with her husband during World War II and was its president for 30 years. Mattel was a successful furniture company first, but it eventually transitioned into toys: making plastic ukuleles, toy pianos, and more. When Mattel began selling Barbies, it would go on to become a multibillion-dollar business. Today, 58 million Barbies are purchased every year and Barbie's line of products is considered the most successful in the history of the toy industry.

141 First Televised Presidential Debate: JFK Outshines Nixon

Americans used to get their news from the radio. In 1950, only 11 percent of Americans had televisions. By 1960, 88 percent of Americans had TVs in their homes.

The first televised presidential debate to air on TV happened on September 26, 1960. Democratic candidate John F. Kennedy and Republican candidate Vice President Richard Nixon debated live from Chicago. Kennedy was only 43 years old and appeared young and vibrant on camera in a blue suit. He talked directly to the camera, captivating millions of American viewers. Nixon was just four years older, but his gray suit blended into the background and made him look tired. He spoke directly to Kennedy—not the camera—so viewers didn't trust him.

Kennedy went on to become the 35th president and the youngest man elected. During Kennedy's time in office, he pushed for getting a man on the moon and equal rights for all Americans. Kennedy was tragically assassinated in Dallas, Texas, in 1963, which also made him the youngest president to die in office.

142 Dolores Huerta & Cesar Chavez: *¡Sí, se puede!*

Dolores Huerta and Cesar Chavez, two Latino activists and civil rights leaders, founded the National Farm Workers Association (NFWA) in 1962. Their goal was to help organize farm workers in the Central Valley of California, which produces a quarter of the nation's food. Huerta and Chavez wanted these workers to get higher wages, health care, safer pesticide-free working environments, and better housing.

The two stayed focused on helping this community, which was made up of Filipino, Mexican, Puerto Rican, Chicano, Black, and white workers. In 1965, Huerta organized a strike of 5,000 workers. All of their hard work led to the California Agricultural Labor Relations Act of 1975, a farm labor law that helped protect workers by giving them the right to organize and negotiate for better wages and working conditions.

143 **The Space Needle:** Seattle's Futuristic World's Fair

The theme of Seattle's 1962 World's Fair was "The Age of Space," so the iconic Space Needle was the perfect monument for the moment. At a sky-high 605 feet (184 m) tall, the Space Needle features a saucer-shaped observation platform with amazing views of the city and Mount Rainier.

A local children's book author wrote a story about Wheedle, an imaginary orange Bigfoot-like character who lives on top of the Space Needle. Wheedle became the mascot for the now-retired NBA Supersonics, Seattle's men's basketball team.

144 **Rita Moreno:** Historic Oscar Win

At the 34th Academy Awards ceremony in 1962, *West Side Story* won ten Oscars, including Best Picture. One of those awards was a history-making win. Puerto Rican actress Rita Moreno won for best supporting actress, the first Hispanic woman to take home an Oscar for acting.

But working after her Oscar win wasn't easy. She was typecast in roles she didn't like, so she decided to act outside of Hollywood. Her hard work paid off. Moreno went on to "EGOT" by the age of 45.

Fun Fact: If someone "EGOTs," it means they've won an Emmy Award, Grammy Award, Oscar Award, and Tony Award. That means they're very talented in TV, music, film, and theater!

145 **The Amazing Spider-Man:** Hero Swings into Comic Book History

Writer Stan Lee's latest work, Spider-Man, was introduced to the world when the comic book *Amazing Fantasy #15* first hit the shelves in 1962. Readers loved new character Peter Parker's double life as a high school student and superhero. He soon starred in his own series, which launched with the comic book *Amazing Spider-Man #1* and explored his crime-fighting abilities and life as a teenager after being bit by a radioactive spider. Today, Spider-Man is one of the world's most popular superheroes with eight live-action movies and two animated features (with more on the way).

146 Dr. Martin Luther King, Jr.: "I Have a Dream"

On August 28, 1963, Dr. Martin Luther King, Jr., the most well-known leader in the Civil Rights Movement, gave a speech that would go down in history. King's "I Have a Dream" speech was given from the steps of the Lincoln Memorial during the March on Washington, a movement that demanded equal rights for Black Americans.

One hundred years after the signing of the Emancipation Proclamation, King spoke of Black Americans still not being free. He spoke of his dream that the nation would honor the words in the Declaration of Independence: that all men are created equal.

King was also known for his nonviolent protests. He organized the Montgomery Bus Boycott in response to Rosa Parks's resistance. He led another protest in Birmingham, Alabama, which was considered the most segregated city in America, where he organized marches, shopping boycotts, and lunch counter sit-ins, where Black people would sit in seats reserved for white people at restaurants.

In 1964, Congress passed the Civil Rights Act, which finally eliminated segregation in America and made discrimination of any kind illegal, whether it was based on race, color, sex, national origin, or religion. Everyone was equally welcome into public places, schools, and workplaces. That same year, King became the youngest person to win the Nobel Peace Prize at age 35 for his nonviolent work against racism. Three years later, he was assassinated in Memphis, Tennessee, as he prepared to lead another peaceful protest march. King is the only non-president to have a national holiday in his honor.

147 The Equal Pay Act: A Women's Rights Movement

In the early 1960s, one-third of working people were women, but they were paid 40 percent less than men. Women had been fighting for equal pay for years. During World War II, many women stepped into the jobs left by men who had traveled abroad to fight in the war, but they were still sometimes paid less. In 1945, a Women's Equal Pay Act was introduced to Congress but never passed.

President John F. Kennedy signed the Equal Pay Act in 1963. The law required that men and women receive equal pay for equal work, which was one of the first laws to address the fact that men and women were treated differently in the workplace based on their gender. When the landmark Civil Rights Act of 1964 was passed, it strengthened this law even more.

148 Julia Child: French Cooking in America

Chef Julia Child is considered the world's first cooking star, and it all started with her new TV show, *The French Chef*, in 1963. Child introduced American audiences to French cooking. Although French cuisine was seemingly fancy, Child was funny, quirky, and six feet three inches tall. Audiences loved her. The show ran for ten seasons.

Child wasn't always good at cooking—in fact, she was bad when she first started! When her husband got stationed in Paris for work, she enrolled in the city's famous cooking school, Le Cordon Bleu. She struggled at first and even failed her first exam, but she fell in love with cooking and eventually graduated. Years later, she'd win many awards, be featured on the cover of *Time* magazine, and create many more popular TV shows and best-selling cookbooks. In 1993, she was the first woman inducted to the Culinary Institute of America's Hall of Fame.

“Beatlemania”: The Beatles Takes Over American Music

An unknown British band called the Beatles took the stage during the popular *The Ed Sullivan Show* on February 9, 1964—and from that moment on, it was “Beatlemania” across the country. Seventy-three million Americans tuned in to that episode, making it the most watched TV event of the time.

The rock ’n’ roll band performed in front of a live audience of screaming teenage girls while they performed hits like “I Want to Hold Your Hand.” John Lennon, Paul McCartney, George Harrison, and Ringo Starr—the “Fab Four”—were instantly household names in America.

When TV host Ed Sullivan was at London’s Heathrow Airport, he had seen thousands of teenage girls screaming when the Beatles arrived. He decided he should book the band on his show even though they were completely unknown in America.

The Beatles went on to record hit after hit, including “Strawberry Fields Forever,” “Hey Jude,” and “Let It Be,” and starred in their own movies like *Yellow Submarine*. Though they were only together for eight years, the Beatles went on to sell 1.6 billion singles in the United States alone, have 20 number one hits on the Billboard charts—more than any other band—and release a record-setting 19 number one albums in the US. Their song “Yesterday” is the most-covered song of all time, with over 3,000 musicians recording their own version of it. The Beatles are considered the biggest and most successful band in history.

Hitsville U.S.A.: Motown Meets the Supremes

The catchy lyrics from the Supremes song "Where Did Our Love Go?" stayed number one on the charts for two weeks in 1964. Diana Ross, Florence Ballard, and Mary Wilson instantly became the country's favorite girl group. Their next release, "Baby Love," also hit number one that year, which made them the first Motown group to have multiple chart-topping songs.

Motown was the name of a famous Black-owned record label. Based in Detroit, Michigan, Motown produced pop and soul hits during the 1960s, and their roster included many Black artists like the Jackson 5 and Stevie Wonder. Owner Barry Gordon placed a sign outside that said "Hitsville U.S.A." because they produced one hit after another. The Supremes alone would go on to have 12 number one hits including, "Stop! In the Name of Love."

Motown changed the music industry forever by creating girl groups, singer-songwriters, and helping Black artists break through to the mainstream culture in America.

Wilderness Act: Protecting & Preserving Land for All

In 1955, a group of environmentalists made headlines when they stopped a dam from being built in Utah. The debate brought national attention to the natural wonders of the US and how to stop humans from destroying them.

When the Wilderness Act was passed in 1964, it established the world's first wilderness system: 54 protected areas across the US. The act is one of the greatest conservation efforts in US history.

These wild areas are open to visitors to explore respectfully and enjoy the peace. "Wilderness" doesn't mean forest—some of these areas are sandy beaches or dry deserts or mountainous meadows. Now there are 803 wilderness areas across more than 100 million acres—from a lagoon in Florida to forests in Alaska.

Patsy Mink: First Female Asian American in Congress

When Patsy Mink was elected to the US House of Representatives in 1964, she was the first Asian American woman and first woman of color to serve in Congress. During her time in Congress, she fought for the rights of women, children, and minorities.

In college, she was only allowed in the dorms for international students. When she wanted to become a doctor, she couldn't—the medical schools wouldn't accept women into their programs. When Mink wanted to start practicing law after college, no one would hire her for being in an interracial marriage and for being a mother. Instead, she opened her own law firm and became the first Japanese American woman to practice law in her home state of Hawaii.

Mink went on to coauthor Title IX (page 110), a groundbreaking equal rights law.

The Gateway Arch: Sightseeing in St. Louis

The Gateway Arch opened in St. Louis in 1965, and visitors began riding the tram 630 feet (192 m) into the air to enjoy the panoramic views of Missouri and Illinois. The stainless-steel structure—the world's tallest arch—extends 60 feet (18 m) into the ground to withstand high winds, lightning strikes, and earthquakes.

A one-of-a-kind tram system—a unique combination of an elevator and a Ferris wheel—was developed to reach the top of the arch in four minutes. There is one train on each side of the arch with eight pods each. The pods rotate like a Ferris wheel as the train moves up the arch. After seeing the observation deck 63-stories high, visitors hop in the same train to ride back down on the same side.

The arch is considered a "gateway to the west" and commemorates Thomas Jefferson's 1803 vision for a growing country and Lewis and Clark's expedition (page 28), which began nearby on the Missouri River in 1804.

154 Daylight Saving Time: Fall Behind, Spring Ahead

Americans change their clocks one hour ahead the second Sunday in March. This is known as Daylight Saving Time—it gives us an extra hour of daylight in the spring and summer. On the first Sunday in November, we change our clocks back one hour to standard time. That's where we get the phrase, "Fall behind, spring ahead!"

The practice of changing the clocks ahead can be traced to saving energy during wars. It wasn't called Daylight Saving Time then—it was called "war time." Since the sun set an hour later, people were more likely to spend time out of their home, shopping and taking part in other recreational activities. Spending money was good for the economy, and being outside an extra hour was good for everyone's health.

Fun Fact: States can opt out of Daylight Saving Time by passing a law—Hawaii and Arizona did!

But farmers didn't like it—it meant they had one less hour of light in the morning to get everything harvested. They lobbied Congress so hard that Daylight Saving Time was stopped before the end of World War I, which meant it only lasted about a year and a half. But New York City kept it going. In fact, many cities did, but the rural areas around them did not. It made it very confusing to coordinate schedules for trains, TV shows, and more.

Daylight Saving Time was introduced again nationwide during World War II from 1942 to 1945, and more confusion followed. In 1966, Congress passed the Uniform Time Act to set a national standard time that everyone had to follow.

155 *Loving v. Virginia:* Interracial Marriage is Legal

In the 1950s, Richard Loving, a white man, and Mildred Jeter, a Black and Native American woman, fell in love in their home state of Virginia. Since interracial marriage was illegal in Virginia, they traveled to nearby Washington, DC, to legally marry in 1958.

Weeks later, the Lovings were arrested. They were sentenced to one year in prison—or to leave Virginia for 25 years. The Lovings moved to DC where they raised three children, but they soon wanted to return home. In 1963, the American Civil Liberties Union (ACLU) offered to help the Lovings.

The *Loving v. Virginia* case made it all the way up to the US Supreme Court. The Supreme Court made an unanimous decision to strike down any existing laws that banned interracial marriage. Declaring interracial marriage laws unconstitutional was a landmark moment in civil rights history and the push for racial equality.

156 The Post-it Note: A Helpful Accident!

In 1968, Dr. Spencer Silver, a scientist, was working in a laboratory. His job as a researcher was to develop superstrong adhesives, or glue—the tougher the better! While researching, he invented the exact opposite—an adhesive that was just a little bit sticky. It could be removed very easily. He thought it was an interesting discovery, but he didn't know how to use it. Years passed, but he couldn't come up with any good ideas for this glue.

In 1974, a fellow scientist named Art Fry used scraps of paper for bookmarks, but the scraps of paper kept falling out. He needed a sticky bookmark that wouldn't ruin the pages of his book—and then he remembered his coworker Silver's discovery.

The two scientists worked together on their idea over the next few years, and they finally landed on the beloved removable sticky note. The Post-it Note was released in stores on April 6, 1980. It became an overnight success—over ten years in the making!

157

Mister Rogers' Neighborhood:

"Won't You Be My Neighbor?"

In the late 1960s in Pittsburgh, Pennsylvania, a man named Fred Rogers recorded the first episode of his new children's television show. As he began singing the lyrics to his theme song, "Won't You Be My Neighbor?," he zipped up his cardigan (hand-knit by his mom), changed into sneakers, and began talking directly to the camera.

Mister Rogers often visited his "Neighborhood of Make Believe" on a red trolley. Inside lived puppets Daniel the Striped Tiger, King Friday, X the Owl, and farmer Donkey Hodie. Rogers believed that even make-believe lands were opportunities to talk to kids very gently about tough issues, like divorce or disabilities, and reminding them that they are special just the way they are.

The show became the first children's show to have a Black actor in a recurring role, François Clemmons as Officer Clemmons. A memorable scene in 1969 helped fight against racism and segregation. In that episode, Mister Rogers and Officer Clemmons both put their bare feet in a kiddie pool to cool down, and Rogers dried off Clemmons feet with a towel afterward.

Mister Rogers' Neighborhood ran for more than 900 episodes over 31 years until 2001, which makes it one of the longest-running TV shows in history.

158

Woodstock Music Festival:

Jimi Hendrix's Most Famous Guitar Solo

In the summer of 1969, half a million young adults gathered in the fields of a dairy farm in upstate New York. The four-day event was called Woodstock Music Festival and would go on to become the most famous music festival in history.

Woodstock promoted a message of unity and peace during a time when many were protesting—against the Vietnam War and in support of the Civil Rights Movement. The concert goers were called "hippies" and were known for rock and folk music, tie-dyed clothes, flowers in their long hair, nonviolent behavior, and anti-war and eco-friendly beliefs.

The music festival wasn't well organized. The location changed at the last minute. Tickets were sold ahead of time, but they didn't have time to install ticket booths, so anyone who showed up could get in free. It ended up raining and getting extremely muddy, and there wasn't much food or water—but the music made up for it.

Some of the most popular bands of the time played at Woodstock. But most remember the final performer, Jimi Hendrix, who closed the festival Monday morning after the rain stopped. He played the "Star Spangled Banner" on his electric guitar, and it's considered one of the most famous versions of the national anthem to ever be recorded.

The United Tribes International Powwow: Gathering Native People

In the late 1960s, North Dakota's Native tribes gathered together for a mission: They hoped to open an institution where Native American families in the Great Plains could further their education and live out their dream careers. The United Tribes Technical College opened in the fall of 1969 in Bismarck—the first of its kind. To celebrate, they held a small powwow, which is an Eastern Algonquian word used to describe a gathering of Native people.

Today, the event is called the United Tribes Technical College International Powwow. As one of the largest powwows in the country, it's a cultural celebration featuring different styles of singing, dancing, drumming, food, and artisan goods from Native tribes in the area. Those include the Turtle Mountain Band of Chippewa Indians, the Standing Rock Sioux Tribe, the Spirit Lake Tribe, and more.

Skilled performers compete in elaborate Native regalia in categories like traditional, grass, jingle dress, fancy, which may involve headdresses, shawls, and ribbons. Thousands of drummers, dancers, and artisans travel to Bismarck every year to enjoy the colorful sights, bold sounds, and proud community at this event.

Sesame Street: Educational TV for Kids

When *Sesame Street* premiered its first episode in 1969, it was the first of its kind: a TV show for kids that helped educate, not just entertain. The creator of the show, Joan Ganz Cooney, wanted all children, regardless of where they lived or what they looked like, to get a preschool-level education. That included learning the ABCs and how to count but also included learning how to be kind and how to care for yourself. At the time, people thought all TV was bad for kids!

People and characters of all backgrounds live together on Sesame Street alongside puppet characters like Oscar the Grouch, Big Bird, Bert and Ernie, Cookie Monster, and Elmo. The puppets, which are called Muppets and were created by famous puppeteer Jim Henson, have become celebrities themselves.

Fun Fact: Elmo's birthday is February 3. Every year, Elmo turns three and a half years old.

161 Man on the Moon: "One Small Step for Man . . ."

In 1961, President John F. Kennedy set a goal: fly a man to the moon and safely return him to Earth. Eight years later on July 16, 1969, three astronauts blasted off on the space shuttle *Apollo 11* from Cape Canaveral, Florida, headed straight for the moon.

Four days later, astronauts Neil Armstrong and Buzz Aldrin climbed inside a smaller lunar module called *Eagle*. It detached from the command center of their spaceship and landed on the moon's surface.

When the *Eagle* touched down, Armstrong announced back to the NASA team in Houston, Texas: "The *Eagle* has landed." Before exiting the vehicle, Armstrong turned on a small black and white camera (that cost over $2 million at the time!) to record live what was about to happen.

At that moment, over 500 million people tuned in to Armstrong's fuzzy live footage on their televisions. As he climbed down the vehicle's ladder and landed on solid ground, he became the first person ever to walk on the moon's surface. His words were remembered forever: "That's one small step for man, one giant leap for mankind."

Aldrin and Armstrong spent almost an entire day on the moon. They conducted experiments to detect solar wind, measure potential "moonquakes," and set up mirrors to reflect lasers shot from Earth. They also gathered samples of lunar rock, planted the American flag on the moon's surface, and took a phone call from President Richard Nixon.

Earth Day: Embracing the Environment

In the 1960s, people became more concerned with pollution and the health of our planet, especially after thousands of gallons of oil accidentally spilled into the Pacific Ocean. Wisconsin Senator Gaylord Nelson organized the first Earth Day in an effort to educate college students about why it's important to care for the environment.

The very first Earth Day took place on April 22, 1970—after spring break but before final exams—and more than 12,000 Earth Day events were attended by millions of Americans around the country.

Starbucks: Opening Day Buzz in Seattle

The very first Starbucks coffee shop opened at the Pike Place Market in Seattle with just one employee manning the counter on March 30, 1971. Its siren-shaped logo could be found outside—as well as a long line—but the iconic mermaid was brown, not green, and she had two tails.

By the 1980s, Starbucks customers had to learn its new "language": instead of small, medium, and large, drinks are tall, grande, venti, and trenta (for extra-large). "Grande" means "large" in Italian while "venti" means 20 and "trenta" means 30, which refers to how many ounces are in each cup.

Title IX: Equal Rights at School and in Sports

In the early 1970s, some colleges only allowed men to apply as students and wouldn't hire female professors. Colleges that did have female students might not let them get a law or medical degree. But when Title IX (say "Title Nine") was passed in 1972, it made sure women had equal access and equal treatment as men.

Title IX also helped increase the popularity of women's sports by requiring equal opportunities and equal funding as men's sports. When the law became required in 1978, six times as many high school girls were playing sports compared to 1970.

165 **Atari:** Gaming Company Launches Pong

Pong, a simple ping-pong-inspired arcade game, changed the gaming industry forever when it was released in 1972 by Atari. It became an instant hit and the first video game to become popular to such a big audience.

The game required two players, which was exciting at the time. The black screen had only three elements: a white ball that bounced between two white rectangular paddles, one controlled by each player. It was simple and easy to understand—and addicting!

Arcade games are stand-alone gaming cabinets that were played by inserting a quarter into the machine. Players stood in front of the cabinet and used simple controls like a joystick or push buttons. They were found in restaurants, bars, and "arcades," which were places with many arcade cabinets. When the first prototype of the coin-operated Pong arcade cabinet was installed at a bar in California, the owner thought the game had broken within a few days. But it turned out it was overflowing with quarters because it was so popular!

166 **Katharine Graham:** First Female CEO

Journalist Katharine Graham's parents became the owners of *The Washington Post*, a daily newspaper business, in 1933. Graham's dad eventually gave the company to her husband. She wasn't the first pick as CEO because she was a woman. When her husband passed away, Graham earned the title of publisher in 1969 then CEO in 1972. This made her the first female CEO of a Fortune 500 company, and the first female publisher of a major newspaper.

Graham is best known for bravely publishing a top-secret document in 1971 called the Pentagon Papers, which outlined the US's military involvement in Vietnam. She felt it should be seen by the American public. The Supreme Court later agreed with her decision. She won the Pulitzer Prize, the top award in journalism, in 1998.

Endangered Species Act: Save the Animals!

During the 1960s and 1970s, it was becoming clear that the actions of humans were harming our planet. Some plant and animal species were dying—and those species would eventually become extinct. Pesticides, hunting, and loss of habitat were just a few reasons why these species were disappearing quickly.

The Endangered Species Act was passed in 1973 to help conserve all kinds of species: plants, animals, fish, insects, and more. The first step was to create a list of endangered species, then make it illegal to collect, harm, or kill these species. The next step was to protect the habitats and ecosystems that those species needed to survive. The act was the biggest conservation law passed in the US. It included more than 1,700 species—half of which were plants.

The act is more than 50 years old now and hundreds of species have been saved from extinction. American alligators, bald eagles, whooping cranes, and peregrine falcons are just some of the animals that could have disappeared from our planet if not for the Endangered Species Act.

Conservationists argue that we should be spending even more money protecting species—especially for the protection of plants. The US continues to spend over $1 billion per year to help support the act, including providing protection for salmon, steelhead trout, grizzly bears, manatees, spotted owls, and more.

168 “Battle of the Sexes”: Billie Jean King Wins for Women

The most-watched tennis match in history happened on September 20, 1973. Bobby Riggs, the world’s best male tennis player, challenged top female tennis player Billie Jean King to a match. The match became known as the “Battle of the Sexes,” and millions of TV viewers tuned in to watch it live.

Although Riggs was 55 years old, he bet that he could beat the top female tennis players of the time even though they were much younger than him. At first, King said no. Margaret Court, another top female tennis player, agreed to play Riggs. She lost—by a lot. That fired up 29-year-old King who then agreed to play Riggs.

King beat Riggs in all three sets and changed women's tennis forever. She went on to create the Women’s Tennis Association and fought for equal opportunities within the sport of tennis. In 1972, she had won the US Open and was only awarded a fraction of what the male winner got. In 1973, male and female winners were awarded equal prize money.

169 Shang-Chi: An Asian Superhero Finds His Fans

Marvel’s first Asian superhero, Shang-Chi, appeared in *Special Marvel Edition* No. 15 on December 1, 1973. He was a Chinese assassin trained by his father, but he realized he’d been fighting for the wrong side and moved to California to change his life. His story started in a limited series, which meant Marvel probably didn’t think it would be that popular—but fans loved Shang-Chi’s story.

To feed fans’ appetites, Marvel created a monthly Shang-Chi comic book series plus special editions. In 2021, a movie called *Shang-Chi and the Legend of the Ten Rings* came out starring actor Simu Liu. It was the first Marvel superhero film with an Asian lead. It smashed box office records and became the biggest Labor Day Weekend opening ever, and one of the top ten highest-earning films of 2021.

170 **The Hollywood Blockbuster:** Lights, Camera, Action!

Lines stretched around the block at theaters across the country in the summer of 1975. Everyone wanted to see Steven Spielberg's latest movie *Jaws*, about a killer shark that terrifies a tiny beach town during the busy summer season. It was the first time a film earned more than $100 million at the box office. *Jaws* ended up becoming the highest-earning movie of 1975 and now holds the Guinness World Record for "First Summer Blockbuster Film."

For months leading up to the release of the film, audiences watched TV commercials and interviews with the actors, and they picked up the novel the film was based on with a new special cover. This marketing bonanza, where audiences became familiar with the movie long before it came out, followed by huge audiences who showed up at the theaters, led to the new term: "blockbuster."

Other movies followed in Spielberg's steps. In 1977, George Lucas was about to release the first movie in his Star Wars trilogy. Lucas wanted to release toys at the same time as the movie, but no toy companies were interested in this new space movie because they didn't believe it would be that popular. Kenner Products finally signed on to make three-inch (8 cm) action figures of the movie's most popular characters. *Star Wars* ended up becoming such a huge success that Kenner had to sell empty toy boxes with coupons for an action figure that would be sent in the mail months later.

171

Grease: "You're the One That I Want"

The movie *Grease* came out in 1978, but it was set in the 1950s with poodle skirts, jukeboxes, and drive-in movie theaters. Based on a Broadway musical of the same name, the movie starred singer Olivia Newton-John as Sandy and actor John Travolta as Danny, two summer-loving teens who are surprised they attend the same high school come fall.

Grease became the highest-grossing musical film of the twentieth century, and the soundtrack had four *Billboard* top ten songs, including "Summer Nights" and "You're the One That I Want." *Grease* still stands as one of the top ten best-selling soundtracks of all time.

172

Hawaiian: The Official Language of Hawaii

Hawaii is the only state in the US with a non-English official language. However, 'Ōlelo Hawai'i, which translates to "Hawaiian language," was banned by the US government in 1896.

In 1978, the state amended the constitution to require the study of Hawaiian history, culture, and language in Hawaiian schools. It also mandated that Hawaiian—not English—was the state's official language. Today, the Hawaiian language is still considered "endangered," which means there are less than 300 native speakers worldwide. But Hawaiian language immersion schools across the islands teach kids from a very young age how to speak their native language.

173

AAPI Heritage: Celebrating Asian & Pacific Islander Americans

In 1979, 39th President Jimmy Carter made an important announcement: Starting that year, a week in May would be dedicated to celebrating Asian and Pacific American culture, history, and people. May commemorates the month that Japanese people first immigrated to the United States in 1843.

In 1992, President George H. W. Bush turned the week-long celebration into a whole month and renamed it AAPI Heritage Month. AAPI celebrates cultures from the entire Asian continent, including Southeast, East, and South Asia plus the Pacific Islands like Polynesia, Melanesia, and Micronesia. Today, about seven percent of the US population identifies as AAPI.

174 Sony Walkman: Introducing Dancing on Your Own

Before July 1, 1979, there was no such thing as "portable music." For most of the 1900s, music was played from a bulky device, called a record player, that had to be plugged into the wall. Before records, people listened to music on the radio, which meant they could never choose what song they wanted to listen to.

When the Sony Walkman was introduced in 1979, it changed everything. It used the much smaller cassette tape to play music. A long, thin ribbon of plastic was wound into each cassette tape, and about 90 minutes of music could be recorded onto each tape. Music lovers could insert a cassette tape into their Sony Walkman, pop on a pair of headphones, and hit play. For the first time ever, people could listen to music or the radio on the go—not just at home or in the car. Headphones meant no one had to know what you were listening to.

In the 1980s, another cassette tape player called the boombox became popular—a larger portable device with big speakers. It allowed people to record songs from the radio onto a blank cassette tape, which inspired people to create mixtapes, or cassette tapes with a mix of their favorite songs. It was like a custom playlist, which is much easier to create today with music streaming services like Spotify and Apple Music!

175 Nickelodeon: First TV Channel for Kids

When Nickelodeon launched in 1979, it was the first cable TV channel for kids showing cartoons and live-action shows. One of their earliest shows, *You Can't Do That on Television,* often slimed the actors by dumping a bucket of green goo on their head. Soon, "getting slimed" became a signature Nickelodeon move.

Nickelodeon had a game show for kids called *Double Dare.* Contestants answered trivia questions and competed in messy obstacle courses, like jumping into a giant bowl of spaghetti, picking a giant nose, or getting covered in slime. Nickelodeon also had a group comedy show called *All That,* which was like *Saturday Night Live* for kids.

Fun Fact: Nickelodeon isn't a totally made-up word. Movie theaters in the early 1900s showed short films for five cents—a nickel!

Since then, Nickelodeon has created tons of shows for kids ages two to 17, with favorites like *Rugrats, Paw Patrol, Carly,* and *SpongeBob SquarePants.*

176 Required Recycling: Woodbury, NJ, Goes Green

In 1980, Woodbury, New Jersey, started a curbside pick-up recycling program and became the first city to require its residents to recycle. City council member Donald Sanderson came up with the idea, and he knew this was a good plan. After all, the landfill where the city dumped their trash was almost full.

At first, residents were not happy—it seemed like a lot of work to sort their trash into different bins. Some residents even threw trash on Sanderson's lawn! But within three months, many of the city residents got into a rhythm and the new recycling program was a huge success. Sanderson even went on to become mayor of the city in 1994. The curbside recycling program was the first in the nation (maybe even the world!). Sanderson ended up teaching other cities around the world how to set up a recycling program. Now, he is known as the "father of recycling."

177 "Miracle on Ice": US Olympic Hockey Team Wins Gold

When the US Olympic hockey team was set to play the Soviet Union hockey team in the semi-finals at the 1980 Olympics, they knew one thing: The Soviets had won gold at the last four Olympics. Everyone expected one outcome—the Soviets would win again. There was seemingly no way Team USA would move on to the next round for a chance to win the gold.

The young Team USA was not considered real competition, but their coach Herb Brooks trained the college kids from Minnesota well. Before the Olympics, Team USA was considered the seventh best team out of the 12 who would compete.

They beat the first five countries they played—but were still considered the underdog. When the semi-final game against the Soviets started in New York, the Soviets quickly scored. Team USA fought back to tie the game 1–1. Minutes later, the Soviets scored for a lead. Then Team USA scored again. It was 2–2.

Overtime kicked in, and they were tied at 3–3. And then Team USA scored once more with ten minutes left in the game. The play-by-play announcer Al Michaels uttered these now-famous words, "Do you believe in miracles? Yes!"

Team USA won 4–3. Their goalie, Jim Craig, stopped the Soviets from scoring 36 times, which is known as one of the greatest goalie performances of all time. Team USA went on to play for the gold medal against Finland—and won 4–2. Announcer Michaels screamed, "This impossible dream comes true!" as the crowds chanted, "USA! USA!"

PETA: Rights for Animals Too!

PETA, which stands for People for the Ethical Treatment of Animals, was founded in 1980 to fight for the rights of animals. PETA believes all animals deserve kindness and respect. Members of PETA fight for a lot of causes, including how animals are treated in laboratories, in the food industry, and in the entertainment business.

Their first campaign released photos of monkeys that were being used as test subjects in a laboratory. The monkeys were rescued, and the owners were punished. Since then, PETA has convinced top fashion brands not to use real animal fur and closed the Barnum & Bailey Circus, which used animals for entertainment in its circus show.

Ronald Reagan: A Movie Star Becomes President

There's something unique about the 40th President Ronald Reagan—before his 1981 inauguration, he used to be a movie star!

Reagan went to Hollywood and did a screen test after being a sportscaster. Warner Brothers signed him as an actor within 48 hours! Reagan acted in more than 50 films from the 1930s to the 1950s, and he was often cast as the leading man in romantic comedies, westerns, and more. His interest in politics started in 1947 when he was elected president of the Screen Actors Guild in Los Angeles and then in 1966 when he was elected governor of California.

Justice O'Connor: Woman on the Supreme Court

When Sandra Day O'Connor was appointed to the Supreme Court in 1981, she became the first woman to ever serve on the highest court in the country—and the Supreme Court had existed for 191 years!

After getting a law degree in 1952, she applied for jobs at law firms. No one would hire her as a lawyer because she was a woman. O'Connor eventually became an Arizona state senator and the first woman to be chosen as the Republican majority leader. She eventually retired from her position on the Supreme Court, and President Barack Obama awarded her with a Presidential Medal of Freedom in 2009.

181 **Sally Ride:** She's Out of This World!

Physicist Sally Ride became the first American woman to travel to space in 1983. Ride was a part of a special group of astronauts called Astronaut Group 8, which was formed in 1978 and was the first group of astronauts that included women and people of color.

On June 18, Ride and four crewmates rocketed into orbit on the space shuttle *Challenger* from the Kennedy Space Center in Florida. They stayed in space for six days. While on board, they deployed two satellites and conducted experiments, including one that investigated space sickness and another that analyzed the effect of zero gravity on the behavior of a colony of carpenter ants. Ride and her crewmates circled Earth 98 times before landing.

After Ride completed a second mission aboard the *Challenger* in 1984, she became a physics professor at the University of California and director of the California Space Institute in Los Angeles. She continued to inspire kids to love science with her programs like Sally Ride Science, which focused on inspiring girls to get involved in science, technology, engineering, and math fields (STEM).

182 **MTV:** The Rise of Music Videos

A 24-hour music TV station called MTV (short for Music Television) debuted in 1981. It played music videos around the clock, which meant people were always discovering new music. The first music video that played on the channel was "Video Killed the Radio Star" by The Buggles. Soon, musicians began spending more time and money on elaborate music videos to go along with each song release, and the music video became like a short film for each song.

> ***Fun Fact:*** MTV also is known for its television shows, like the reality show *Jersey Shore* and the comedy show *Ridiculousness*, both full of crazy viral moments.

In 1992, MTV launched the MTV Video Music Awards (VMAs) to recognize the best music videos. The winner is given a "Moonman" trophy, which is an astronaut holding an MTV flag. The VMAs often have iconic celebrity moments, like when Beyoncé announced her pregnancy after performing live.

183 **The Statue of Liberty Disappears:** David Copperfield's Major Illusion

Can you imagine Lady Liberty disappearing right before your eyes? Magician David Copperfield made the Statue of Liberty disappear on live TV in 1983. Besides the millions watching from home, an audience of 20 people sat right in front of the statue. A curtain went up. When it dropped, Lady Liberty was gone.

It was an illusion that tricked millions (the 62,000-pound [28 tons] statue didn't really disappear!) and went on to get listed in the Guinness Book of World Records as the "largest illusion ever staged." Even the US government had to agree to the illusion. They granted Copperfield permission to pull it off.

The secret to the illusion—a feat of engineering and sneakiness—wasn't revealed until decades later. Two towers had been set up next to the statue to hold the curtain. When the curtain was closed, the platform with the live audience (and the cameras) very slowly rotated until the statue was hidden behind one of the towers. When the curtain dropped, the statue appeared to be gone. Clever lighting tricks also helped!

Macintosh: Apple's First Computer

Steve Jobs inserted a floppy disc into a small beige box during a meeting in 1984, and the word "Macintosh" appeared on the box's tiny screen. It was a personal computer unlike anything anyone had ever seen.

The Apple Macintosh 128k was smaller than other computers at the time—most were as big as a cabinet! The advertising said it could be "carried in a bag." In some ways, it looked similar to today's personal computers. It had a mouse and a screen, menus and folders, and a trash can icon. But it cost $2,495 (which is equivalent to more than $7,000 today!).

The computer wasn't a big success, and Jobs got fired from Apple, the company he started in his garage in 1976. (He would eventually come back to Apple in 1997.) But it was popular with creative people, and it became one of the most important computers in history. It was a computer with personality that was designed for the average person at home, which had always been Jobs's goal when he dreamed up ideas in his garage.

The Macintosh weighed around 16 pounds (7 kg), which is around the weight of a bowling ball. Now, a MacBook Air weighs just under three pounds (1 kg).

185 Gymnast Mary Lou Retton: Perfect Score

At the 1984 Olympics in California, Mary Lou Retton became the first American gymnast to win a gold medal for the all-around competition. Retton scored two back-to-back perfect scores, a 10, which was the highest score a gymnast could earn at the time.

She blew everyone's mind when she took to the floor exercise and scored the first perfect 10. Next was vault, and the only way she'd win gold is if she scored yet another perfect 10. She did a difficult vault called a double Tsukahara—and stuck the landing. A perfect 10.

Gymnasts are allowed to perform twice on the vault and take the highest of the two scores. Even though she couldn't improve on a 10, she tried again anyway—and got her third perfect 10. Retton went on to score four more medals during the team and individual competitions. With five medals, she had won more medals than any other athlete at the Olympic Games that year.

186 American Girl: Introducing Kirsten, Samantha & Molly

American Girl was created in 1986 by former teacher and textbook author Pleasant Rowland in Madison, Wisconsin. She invested $1.2 million of her own money to create a line of three dolls that celebrated different eras in American history—the pioneer era, the turn of the century, and World War II (Kirsten, Samantha, and Molly, respectively). Each doll came with historically accurate clothing and accessories and a set of six books that detailed each character's story.

Many people didn't believe in Rowland's idea—they thought the dolls were too expensive and that girls wouldn't be interested. She sent out 500,000 catalogs in the fall of 1986 and crossed her fingers. Then the phones started ringing. Between September and December of that year, she sold $1.7 million dollars of dolls, accessories, and books. Her investment paid off! The company went on to be wildly successful and sold to Mattel.

187 Aretha Franklin: "Queen of Soul"

When *Rolling Stone* magazine released a list of the 100 greatest singers of all time, Aretha Franklin won the number one spot. The "Queen of Soul" is most known for her gospel-inspired hits of the 1960s, which R&B artists are still inspired by today.

One hundred of Franklin's songs appeared on the Billboard charts, starting with "Respect" in 1967 when she was 24 years old. Her sisters sang backup for her on the song. The lyrics, "R-E-S-P-E-C-T," became a feminist rallying cry at the time and resonated with the civil rights movement too.

"Respect" was a cover of musician Otis Redding's song, which had come out two years before. Audiences fell in love with Aretha's voice and quickly dubbed her, "Lady Soul." The song became number one and won Franklin her first two Grammys. They were for best solo female R&B performance and best R&B recording—and she went on to win these two categories at the Grammys every year for the next eight years.

In 1987, Franklin became the first woman to get inducted in the Rock and Roll Hall of Fame, which is a museum you can visit in Cleveland, Ohio. Today, more than 65 women have been inducted into the Rock and Roll Hall of Fame.

Franklin sang at many famous moments in history, including at the inauguration of President Barack Obama in 2009 and at the memorial service for Dr. Martin Luther King, Jr.

188 "Just Do It": Nike Airs Iconic Slogan

It's hard to believe that there was a time that Nike existed before the "Just do it" slogan. In 1988, a new advertising firm called Wieden and Kennedy took on its first client: Nike, a small running-shoe brand based in Oregon that needed some help developing commercials. They wanted to attract average Americans—not just elite athletes—to their shoe brand.

Dan Wieden created five different commercials for Nike. At the last minute, he decided the commercials needed a tagline to help connect them. Wieden came up with the "Just do it" slogan overnight. Nike and Wieden didn't love the phrase, but they gave it a try anyway.

The 30-second commercial featured an 80-year-old man running across the Golden Gate Bridge in San Francisco saying, "I run 17 miles (27 km) every morning." And then the phrase "Just do it" flashed on the screen. "Just do it" became a rallying cry for athletes to push through the hard times.

Fun Fact: Carolyn Davidson, a graphic designer, created the iconic Nike swoosh in 1971. She was paid $35 for her day's work.

With the tagline "Just do it," Nike released three of their most popular shoes ever, including the Air Jordan. Nike went on to become the world's biggest athletic footwear brand—and Wieden and Kennedy went on to become pretty famous too. Advertising Age named "Just do it" the second most famous slogan of the twentieth century, right behind "A diamond is forever."

189 Linda Alvarado: MLB's First Female Owner

When Linda Alvarado became co-owner of the Colorado Rockies in 1991, she was the first woman (and the first Hispanic person) to ever bid on and buy a Major League Baseball team.

In 1976, she started her own construction business called Alvarado Construction. The banks wouldn't give her a loan because they thought investing in a female contractor was too risky. Her parents gave her a small loan and she went on to build one of the most successful construction firms in the country—and she became the first female CEO of a construction company. Her company built the Denver Broncos' Mile High Stadium, a downtown aquarium, and the Denver Botanic Gardens.

190 Mall of America: Shop 'Til You Drop

In 1992, America's largest mall opened in Minnesota with over 300 stores. One lap around the mall is over one mile (2 km) long, and it's seven times the size of Yankee Stadium. In the middle is an amusement park the size of five football fields with indoor roller coasters and rides. There's an aquarium too!

Even though Minnesota is very cold in the winter, the mall doesn't have a central heating system—it stays at a comfortable 70 degrees all year by using solar energy, skylights, light fixtures, and body heat. The mall is also home to 30,000 live plants that help purify the air.

191 Beanie Babies: Collecting Critters

At the 1993 World Toy Fair, a new collection of $5 stuffed animals was introduced to the world: Beanie Babies. The original nine Beanie Babies included Legs the Frog and Squealer the Pig. Each stuffie had a red heart-shaped tag with a name, birthday, and poem inside.

Beanie Babies were an instant hit. Then the toy company began retiring Beanie Babies, which meant you couldn't buy certain characters anymore—and collectors went crazy. Rare Beanie Babies were being sold for $5,000 or more on a new resale website that had launched that year called eBay. By the year 2000, the Beanie Baby craze had died down.

192 ***Jurassic Park:*** Bringing Dinosaurs to Life

When director Steven Spielberg released *Jurassic Park* in 1993, it was the first time human actors interacted with computer-generated characters—in this case, dinosaurs! *Jurassic Park* revolutionized how filmmakers could use special effects, and how they could mix computer-generated images with live-action footage to make fantasies come to life. There were scenes where human actors ran away from a *T. rex* or got sneezed on by a *Brachiosaurus*. Filmmaking would never be the same again.

The star of the movie was the *T. rex*, which was computer animated in some scenes, but in others it was a real-life model the actors could interact with on set. The filmmakers created a lifelike remote-controlled, 25-foot-tall (8 m), and 15,000-pound (7 tons) animatronic model of a *T. rex*. Sometimes while on set, the *T. rex* model turned on by itself and started moving, which made the people on set scream!

Jurassic Park went on to become the highest-grossing film of all time (at the time). A *Jurassic Park* ride opened at Universal Studios Hollywood in California in 1996 and was the most expensive thrill ride ever created. It went on to open at Universal Studios in Orlando, Florida, and Universal Studios Japan in Osaka too. Today, there are two more *Jurassic Park* movies as well as four (and possibly more!) movies in the Jurassic World series.

Connie Chung: First Asian News Anchor

On a Thursday evening in 1993, the CBS Evening News opened with well-known news anchor Dan Rather . . . and a history-making coanchor sitting by his side. As a Chinese American woman, Connie Chung became the first Asian person to anchor a major news network. It was a dream she had been working toward for a long time. She also became the second woman to anchor a nationally televised news show after Barbara Walters.

She was known for her tough interview style and had even interviewed President Richard Nixon during the Watergate scandal—a web of political scandals during President Nixon's term—early in her career. Chung often had to deal with gender discrimination in journalism, often being asked to report on "lighter" stories like fashion while male reporters were asked to cover challenging topics like wars. Chung anchored other news shows including the *NBC Nightly News, 20/20, Good Morning America*, and *Connie Chung Tonight*. She paved the way for future female journalists.

Amazon: Bezos Launches an Online Bookshop

When computer scientist and engineer Jeff Bezos launched his now-infamous website Amazon in the summer of 1994, it looked a lot different than it does today. First, it was called "Cadabra" (like "abracadabra"). Second, it only sold books. Those books were stored in his garage in Washington, ready to ship to customers. He quickly changed the name to Amazon, after the South American river of the same name.

By September, Amazon was selling $20,000 worth of books per week to every state in the country. At the time, it was one of the first websites to sell something over the internet. Bezos thought books made sense to sell online since a mail-order catalog listing every book ever made would be far too heavy to print or ship! The website continued to sell only books until 1999, and then Amazon became a website where you could order anything you could imagine—and it could ship to your home very fast.

Fun Fact: Jeff Bezos also runs Blue Origin, an aerospace company that develops reusable rockets and plans to bring humans to the moon again. He sent pop star Katy Perry to space in 2025!

195 Selena's Best Album: Tejano Music Takes America

Selena, a famous Mexican American musician, is known as the "Queen of Tejano music" or "la Reina de la Onda Tejano." Selena was born in Texas in 1971. When she was as young as six years old, Selena sang at her family's restaurant. Her dad taught her how to sing in Spanish, although they spoke English at home.

Selena's dad decided to create a family band called Selena y Los Dinos. Selena sang the lead, her brother A. B. was on bass, and her sister Suzette was on drums. They played Mexican, country, and Western music in Spanish and English.

Music producers noticed and signed Selena as a solo artist in 1989. She recorded many more albums and recorded songs in both English and Spanish. Her brother helped her write songs. She began taking Spanish lessons in 1990 and soon became fluent so she could speak to the Spanish-speaking crowds at her concerts.

In 1994, Selena won a Grammy award for Best Mexican American Album in 1994 for *Live*. When she was in the middle of recording her next album, Selena tragically passed away. Fans around the world were devastated at the loss.

Selena's brother helped remix some of her most popular songs to finish the bilingual album she had been working on. *Dreaming of You* was released a few months later and was instantly a massive success. Selena became the first Hispanic singer to have an album debut at number one in the US and it stayed there for more than ten months.

196 White House Website: Dot Com for the First Family

The White House got its very first website in 1994 during 42nd President Bill Clinton's administration. At the time, only about ten percent of Americans had internet access!

The simple landing page said, "Welcome to the White House" and had links to a welcome message from the president and Vice President Al Gore, information on tours of the White House, and fun facts about the First Family. When users clicked through, they could find a photo of President Clinton playing the saxophone and posing with Sox, the family cat. There was even an audio clip of Sox the cat!

First Lady Hilary Rodham Clinton's page also included an audio clip. In the clip, she asked what website visitors thought of "this service." Vice President Al Gore's page included his collection of cartoons—any time someone drew a picture of him in a newspaper, he kept it.

197 Denver Airport: North America's Largest Airport

The city of Denver is about 155 square miles (401 sq km)—and one-third of that square mileage is the Denver airport! The Denver International Airport opened in 1995 and became the biggest airport in North America and the second largest in the world after King Fahd International Airport in Saudi Arabia.

Planes flying into Denver can land on the longest commercial runway in North America, which is more than three miles (5 km) long. This extra length is helpful for takeoffs because of Denver's high elevation and summer heat.

The airport has a unique white-peaked roof. It's meant to mimic the Native American teepees that once dotted the region as well as the nearby snow-capped Rocky Mountains.

Toy Story: First Computer-Animated Film

198

Before Pixar's *Toy Story* came out in 1995, every animated film and cartoon short had been entirely drawn by hand. That means 24 drawings were needed for every one second of film. A 90-minute movie could need 129,600 drawings!

In the late 1980s and early 1990s, Disney was interested in using technology to improve their animation process. They asked Pixar, an up-and-coming studio owned by Steve Jobs, for help. Pixar helped by adding computer-generated imagery (CGI) to a hand-drawn scene, like with the magic carpet character in *Aladdin*. The ballroom dance scene in *Beauty and the Beast* also uses some computer animation techniques.

Toy Story, on the other hand, was the first fully computer-animated movie ever made. When the computer scientists and engineers were developing the 3D animation software, they noticed it made everything look plastic-like. So, Pixar decided to create a movie that featured plastic things—toys—and completely avoid humans. (Eventually, they decided they had to show some human faces, including their owner Andy and the frightening Sid.)

Toy Story went on to be a huge hit and won an Academy Award for Special Achievement (in computer animation). The Oscar for Best Animated Feature didn't even exist at the time, but *Toy Story* changed the animation industry forever.

Titanic: A Hollywood Blockbuster

The 1997 movie *Titanic* was about the real-life ocean liner of the same name, which tragically sank in the Atlantic Ocean in 1912. The real-life RMS *Titanic* was the largest ship of its time—and everything about the movie was massive too.

At the time, *Titanic* was the most expensive film ever made—$200 million dollars—and included a lot of special effects. It included underwater footage of the real *Titanic* shipwreck, which director James Cameron filmed himself for 21 days.

Titanic went on to become the number one movie in North America for 15 weeks straight. It stayed in the theaters for almost ten months, which meant fans could buy the VHS tape in stores and bring it home to watch while it was still in theaters. It tied a record for most Oscar nominations and for most Oscar wins when it earned 11 Academy Awards, including Best Picture.

Google: Search the Internet for Anything

In 1996, two Stanford University college students built a search engine in their dorm room that could better organize internet search results. They created an algorithm that ranked pages based on how many other websites linked back to it. They called it "Backrub"—but soon changed the name to Google. It was a play on the word "googol:" the number one followed by 100 zeros.

In 1998, a tech company invested in Google with a $100,000 check, and the students, Larry Page and Sergey Brin, upgraded from the dorm to a garage.

Today, Google continues to run the world's most-used search engine. In 2020, they launched a "hum to search" feature for when you can't think of the song name. You can sing, whistle, or hum a tune to find what you're looking for.

They're also known for their amazingly fun offices that have free food, bowling alleys, climbing walls, nap pods, slides, and more.

201 Michael Jordan & the Chicago Bulls:
All We Do is Win, Win, Win

During game six of the 1998 NBA Finals, the Utah Jazz were in the lead 86–85. But then Chicago Bulls superstar Michael Jordan stole the ball from Jazz player Karl Malone, took a 20-foot-high (6 m) jump, and with only five seconds left scored a two-pointer to win the game 87–86. It was the last shot Jordan, who is considered the greatest basketball player of all time, made for the Chicago Bulls. It was the end of an era for the NBA.

The Bulls won three NBA titles in a row from 1991 to 1993—their first "three-peat"—and then again from 1996 to 1998. After the first "three-peat," 31-year-old Jordan retired from basketball and announced he was playing baseball instead. His minor league baseball stint ended up being a short-lived distraction. On March 18, 1995, he made a simple two-word announcement to the press: "I'm back." To the utter delight of fans, Jordan returned to the Chicago Bulls and the second history-making "three-peat" had begun.

In 1985, Nike released Air Jordans: red, black, and white high-top sneakers. Jordan wore them at every game that season—even though the NBA had deemed the shoe inappropriate and fined him $5,000 per game. Nike happily paid the fine! By 1988, the Air Jordan 3 included Jordan's signature "Jumpman" logo, a silhouette of the famous basketball player leaping through the air for a slam dunk. Today, Air Jordans are one of the most famous shoe brands in the world.

202 Pokémon: It's Raining Pikachus in Topeka

On August 27, 1998, Topeka, Kansas, was renamed "ToPikachu" for the day. It was the first day *Pokémon* arrived in the United States—and they arrived in style. The hand-held video game had debuted in Japan in 1996 and was an instant hit! It was soon followed by the Pokémon Trading Card Game and the anime TV series *Pokémon*. By 1998, the Japanese game maker, Nintendo, thought US audiences were ready to meet Pikachu.

English-speaking versions of the video games, *Pokémon: Red Version* and *Pokémon: Blue Version*, plus the anime TV series were scheduled to launch in the US in September. To introduce American kids to these new characters, they decided to have a Pokémon-themed bonanza in the middle of the country . . . in a city that already sounded kind of like Pikachu.

Fun Fact: Did you know "*Pokémon*" is short for "pocket monsters"? The word was created using a Japanese process known as "*wasei eigo*," where parts of English words are combined to sound more like Japanese.

That day, 700 stuffed Pikachus were dropped from the air in Topeka, each wearing a parachute, to thousands of kids waiting in a field below. Kids learned the phrase, "Gotta catch 'em all!" for the first time.

It turned out American kids loved catching different characters and the themes of adventure and friendship just as much as Japanese kids did. The anime TV show went on for 26 seasons over 1,200 episodes and inspired more than 20 movies that follow ten-year-old Ash Ketchum's adventures as a Pokémon trainer.

203 Women's World Cup Final: Brandi Chastain's Historic Kick

More than 90,000 fans filled the sold-out Rose Bowl stadium in Pasadena, California, for the final game of the 1999 FIFA Women's World Cup. The US Women's National Team was so close to winning its second World Cup. But it all hinged on Brandi Chastain's penalty kick.

She kicked the ball—and it flew right past China's goalie, Gao Hong. The crowd went wild! Chastain ripped off her jersey and fell to her knees to celebrate. In that moment, one of the most iconic photos in sports was captured and later featured on the cover of *Sports Illustrated.*

This World Cup was a huge step forward in women's sports. It was the most successful Women's World Cup with the most people attending and watching live on TV. The final game became the most attended women's sports event in history. And, for the first time, all the referees were women too.

204 You Have Now Arrived: GPS Available for All

Global Positioning System (GPS) is used by Americans every day. It allows mobile devices to know the time, look up directions, and share our location.

It all started in 1957 when Russia launched the satellite, *Sputnik,* into space. Scientists noticed *Sputnik*'s radio signal frequency increased as it got closer to Earth and decreased when it got farther away. They could determine *Sputnik*'s location based on the radio signal. Could they reverse that idea to determine someone's location based on how far they were from *Sputnik*? Turns out, the answer is yes!

The US military began using the satellite navigation technology and launched 36 more satellites into the sky in the 1960s. In 2000, President Bill Clinton opened up the GPS technology to everyone with pinpoint accuracy—GPS could locate anything between two feet to six feet (61 cm to 2 m) most of the time.

Fun Fact: Did you know it takes three satellites to determine your location at any time? The first measures your longitude, the second your latitude, and the third calculates the time—basically your time and place!

2000–2026

The Future Is Now!

205

After the Twin Towers Fell:

FDNY's Largest Rescue Operation

On the morning of September 11, 2001, Chief Joseph Pfeifer of the Fire Department of the City of New York (FDNY) was working on the streets of Manhattan when he heard a loud roar up above. He looked up to see a plane crash into the North Tower of the Twin Towers, two 110-floor skyscrapers that were part of the World Trade Center complex.

Along with members of FDNY, he headed to the North Tower to begin to rescue people inside the building. When the Twin Towers were built in 1974, they were the tallest buildings in the world. Thousands of people could fit into each building, which meant a lot of people needed to be saved from the fire and smoke. Minutes later, a second plane crashed into the South Tower. Less than an hour later, the South Tower collapsed. About 30 minutes later, the North Tower collapsed.

Firefighters from 75 different firehouses around the city came to the Twin Towers to help rescue lives that day. In total, the FDNY saved more than 25,000 people, which makes it the largest rescue operation in US history. Sadly, 343 heroic FDNY firefighters sacrificed their lives while helping others. The phrase "Never Forget" was coined to help remember the fallen first responders who helped that day, as well as the thousands of people who lost their lives in the towers.

206 2001 World Series: Bush's First Pitch

Seven weeks after the attack on 9/11, 43rd President George W. Bush threw out the ceremonial first pitch during game three of the World Series between the New York Yankees and the Arizona Diamondbacks at Yankee Stadium in New York.

The president wore a FDNY pullover with a bulletproof vest underneath. The president waited for game three of the Series to come to New York even though the games in Arizona may have been safer. The Yankees ended up winning that night. President Bush's attendance at the game was an important signal to America that life could go on.

207 *American Idol*: Millions Vote . . . One Wins

Starting in June of 2002, a group of aspiring singers from around the country performed each week in front of a panel of judges on *American Idol*. What was unique about this show was that TV viewers got to decide who won the competition. Viewers could vote for their favorite contestant via text message or phone call. Whoever got the least number of votes was booted off the show each week.

In its first season, 20-year-old Kelly Clarkson won . . . and went on to win three Grammys and released pop hits like "Since U Been Gone."

208 Oprah Winfrey: You Get a Billion, You Get a Billion

Oprah Winfrey is a journalist, media mogul, and businesswoman. At age 32, she became the first African American nationally syndicated talk show host with her popular daytime TV show, *The Oprah Winfrey Show*. The show ran for 25 years! Oprah was famous for giving gifts to her live audience. In one episode in 2004, every audience member was gifted a car!

When Oprah launched Harpo Productions in 1986, she became the first Black person to control their own major studio. In 2003, Oprah became the first Black female billionaire in America.

Mars: Rovers *Spirit* & *Opportunity* Arrive

Humans may not be able to travel to Mars yet, but robots certainly can. NASA sent two twin rovers, *Spirit* and *Opportunity*, to explore Mars in 2004. Rovers have wheels and can drive around to different spots on the red planet's surface. Most importantly, they gather information and take photos to send back to Earth.

At 374 pounds (170 kg), *Spirit* and *Opportunity* were designed to spend a lot of time on Mars. The solar-powered rovers discovered that long-standing water was once on Mars, which made some scientists believe that there may have been life on Mars at one point. *Spirit* sent information from Mars for six years. *Opportunity* lasted for 14 years (and drove a record-setting 28 miles [45 km]!).

Fun Fact: The rover *Curiosity* sang "Happy Birthday" to itself every year on August 5.

Each rover has gotten bigger, heavier, faster, and more capable of finding information and sharing it with us back on Earth. It might help us answer the question: Could humans ever live on Mars?

Social Network: Mark Zuckerberg Starts TheFacebook

In 2004, Harvard sophomore Mark Zuckerberg and four of his friends wanted to create a website that would help Harvard students connect with one another. Users could also post messages and upload photos. He called it TheFacebook and launched it from his dorm room on February 4. Within 24 hours, more than 1,000 students had signed up.

The website continued to grow faster than Zuckerberg could have ever imagined. By spring, TheFacebook was available at all the Ivy League schools and then college campuses around the country. In September 2006, anyone over the age of 13 could sign up for Facebook, and by 2009, it was the most popular social networking service in the world. In 2024, Facebook had over three billion users around the world.

Zuckerberg became the world's youngest multibillionaire. He and his wife, Priscilla Chan, formed a nonprofit that aims to eliminate disease, improve education, and help their local San Francisco Bay Area community.

211 "Me at the zoo": YouTube's First Video

On April 23, 2005, the first video ever was uploaded to a new website called YouTube. The 18-second video was called "Me at the zoo." It was uploaded by YouTube cofounder Jawed Karim—and he's never uploaded another video since. "Me at the zoo" has over 344 million views.

Karim stands by the elephants at the San Diego Zoo and says, "The cool thing about these guys is that they have really, really, really long trunks and that's really cool. And that's pretty much all there is to say."

One year after posting this video, Karim and his cofounders Steven Shih Chen and Chad Hurley sold YouTube to Google for over one billion dollars. YouTube came to be because the founders were curious if they could watch and share videos on a browser without having to download them. They never imagined that it would quickly become the platform that could host all the videos on the internet.

Today, "creator" is a real-life profession, and people can make millions posting videos to the site. Jimmy Donaldson, known as MrBeast, has the most subscribers on YouTube—he has over 400 million subscribers. He's known for his viral challenges and stunts like "Last to Leave Circle Wins $500,000," "I Built Willy Wonka's Chocolate Factory," and "I Survived 100 Hours in an Ancient Temple."

212 Kingda Ka: Fastest Roller Coaster in the World

Would you ride the world's tallest and fastest roller coaster? In 2005, Kingda Ka set both records when it opened at Six Flags Great Adventure in Jackson, New Jersey. The upside-down U-shaped coaster launched riders from 0 to 128 miles per hour (206 km/hr) in less than four seconds. Riders climbed 45 stories, or 456 feet (139 m), at breakneck speed up into the sky at a 90-degree angle and then quickly back down again. The whole ride took just 28 seconds.

Five years later, Kingda Ka lost the record for fastest roller coaster when Formula Rossa opened at Ferrari World in Abu Dhabi, United Arab Emirates. The similar launch coaster hit speeds of almost 150 miles per hour (241 km/hr), but Kingda Ka kept the record for tallest coaster. In 2024, after 12 million people had braved Kingda Ka, Six Flags announced that it would be shutting down and demolishing the much-loved coaster. But they plan to make room for a brand-new multi-world-record-setting roller coaster.

213 Netflix: Movies in Your Mailbox

Today, you can watch any movie on Netflix with just the click of a button. But when the company started in 1998, it sent DVDs to users in the mail. A DVD is a five-inch (13 cm) disc that stores movies or music and can be played on a television or computer. At the time, people were used to renting movies at movie rental stores, like a popular chain called Blockbuster. The movie had to be returned within a couple days or they'd be fined. That meant two trips to the store just to watch one movie!

Users who subscribed to Netflix could select a movie from the website. Then, a disc would show up directly at their house in a slim red envelope. The best part? There were no due dates or late fees. Whenever they were done, they mailed the DVD back.

But the introduction of streaming in 2007 made "renting" movies even easier. Now movie lovers can instantly watch their favorite films and shows—no waiting for the mail to arrive! They've come a long way from the little red envelope.

iPhone: Everything at Your Fingertips

In 2007, when Apple CEO Steve Jobs introduced the iPhone for the first time, a "phone with internet" was a huge deal—it meant the ability to make calls, check email, send text messages, get directions, take photos, and browse the internet all on one device!

The first iPhone cost $499 and was the first phone to have a large three-and-a-half-inch (9 cm) touchscreen that you could tap, slide, drag, and pinch. It also had a virtual keyboard, like one you'd find on a computer, which made it easier than ever to text or email. The iPhone also allowed people to combine their phone and their music player into one device. In 2001, Apple had introduced a portable music player called the iPod. The iPhone could play music and more!

Apple introduced the updated iPhone (which was half the price) in 2008 as well as the App Store, which allowed users to personalize their phones. Three million iPhones were sold in the first month. The iPhone became known as the coolest smartphone.

The iPhone 4 was released in 2010 and looked more like the iPhones of today with the introduction of video calls and a front-facing camera. "Selfies" and "FaceTime" were introduced to Americans' vocabulary for the first time. Today, more than 40 versions of the iPhone have been released. It's considered one of the most popular phones in the world and one of the best-selling products of all time.

215 The Bald Eagle: Saved from Extinction

The bald eagle has a symbol of the United States since 1782. But by 1940, the bald eagle was facing extinction.

The Endangered Species Act (page 112) allowed people to begin work to help save the bald eagle. Conservations started breeding programs in captivity, worked on reintroducing these captive birds to the wild, and protected the nests of bald eagles in the wild during breeding season. In 2007, the bald eagle was removed from the endangered species list. Now, there are thousands of nesting pairs—a conservation success story!

216 Nancy Pelosi: First Female Speaker of the House

When Nancy Pelosi was elected the 52nd Speaker of the House of Representatives, she made history—she was the first woman to do it. The speaker of the house ranks third in charge of the US government, following the president and vice president. That meant she held the title for woman with the highest elected office in the US at the time.

The Democrat from California has fought for fair pay and equal treatment for women and helped pass an act that helped people more easily pay for doctor visits, illnesses, or injuries. She was awarded the Presidential Medal of Freedom in 2024 by President Joe Biden.

217 LeBron James: His First NBA Finals

Game five of the 2007 NBA Eastern Conference Finals between the Detroit Pistons and the Cleveland Cavaliers was a nail-biter. Cleveland had lost the first two games. Then won the second two games. Now it was time for game five.

With just six minutes left in the game and having scored only 19 points, LeBron James made up for lost time. In double overtime, James scored and dunked 29 of Cleveland's 30 points. He nailed a layup with two seconds left to clinch the double overtime win 109–107. James's game five performance went down in history.

218 **Barack Obama:** First African American President

On November 4, 2008, the first African American person was elected president. Barack Obama was a president of many firsts: the first African American to run for president, the first to win, the first president from Hawaii, and the first president to be born after the country had 50 states. His wife, First Lady Michelle Obama, became the first African American to hold her title as well. Obama, a senator from Illinois, was an unlikely candidate to win the election. But his campaign rallying cry of "Yes, we can," and his themes of hope and change resonated with American audiences.

During his presidency, Obama helped Americans afford health care, battled terrorism, and fought for peace. In 2009, he became the fourth president to win the Nobel Peace Prize. Obama also appointed two female Supreme Court Justices, Elena Kagan and Sonia Sotomayor (page 145), which meant the Supreme Court had three female justices for the first time ever.

During his two terms in office, Obama became known for eloquent speeches. During the election, he inspired voters with quotes like, "We are the ones we've been waiting for. We are the change that we seek."

Michelle, a lawyer and graduate from both Princeton University and Harvard Law School, worked hard to bring healthier food to schools, get kids moving, and fight for the rights of girls around the world to receive education.

219 Justice Sotomayor: Supreme Court's First Woman of Color

Justice Sonia Sotomayor was the first Latina, first Hispanic, and the third woman to serve on the US Supreme Court once she stepped into her new role on August 8, 2009. She is of Puerto Rican descent and grew up in public housing in New York City.

During her career, she became known as the judge who "saved" Major League Baseball when she sided with the baseball players to help end a strike about their salaries before opening day of the 1995 MLB season. She helped legalize same sex marriage in all 50 states and twice upheld the Affordable Care Act, which gives Americans access to affordable health care.

220 Michael Phelps: Bringing Home the Gold

At the 2008 Summer Olympic Games in China, American swimmer Michael Phelps won a record-setting eight gold medals—and all eight wins set an Olympic or world record. (Seven were world records!) It was the most gold medals won in a single Olympics.

Phelps made his Olympic debut in Australia when he was just 15 years old. He went on to win 28 medals across five Olympics. He's the most decorated athlete in the history of the Olympic Games and has won the most gold medals. He has 23!

221 SpaceX: Elon Musk Successfully Launches *Falcon 1*

In September of 2008, *Falcon 1* became the first non-NASA rocket to reach Earth's orbit. The successful launch, on the fourth try, led SpaceX to get funding from NASA and continue on their mission to create fully reusable rockets that can carry people to Mars one day.

Rockets usually fly just once, which makes space travel very expensive. But SpaceX has designed rockets that can land and be used again. The 15-story-tall *Falcon 9* rocket was the first rocket to go into orbit and then land vertically back on Earth after launch. It's now parked outside the SpaceX headquarters in California.

222 Captain Sully: "Miracle on the Hudson"

US Airways pilot Chesley "Sully" Sullenberger (left) performed a miracle shortly after takeoff from New York's LaGuardia airport on January 15, 2009. The plane's two engines lost power when it crossed paths with a flock of large Canada geese. With only minutes to act, Captain Sullenberger safely guided the plane to an emergency water landing in the frigid Hudson River, and all 155 people on board survived.

Captain "Sully" became an instant American hero, and the entire crew was applauded for their acts of bravery and heroism. The pilot went on to write a *New York Times* best-selling book about his life that was turned into a movie called *Sully*, starring Tom Hanks as Captain Sullenberger.

Sullenberger learned to fly at age 16, while he was still in high school. He graduated college from the US Air Force Academy and became a fighter pilot in the Air Force before joining US Airways as a pilot. As a flight safety expert, he speaks around the world about air travel safety.

The exact plane from that historic day, an Airbus 320, now resides at the Sullenberger Aviation Museum in Charlotte, North Carolina, an aviation and aerospace history museum named after the famed pilot.

223 International Space Station:
Around the World in 90 Minutes

The International Space Station (ISS) is a working laboratory that orbits through space. More than 270 astronauts (158 of which were American) have visited the station since 1998 to conduct experiments on their own bodies to learn how humans react to life in space. These astronauts also discover new ways to grow plants in harsh conditions and perform other microgravity experiments that can help prepare humans to head back to the moon or elsewhere.

The ISS wasn't fully completed until 2011, though astronauts lived aboard during the construction process. Different parts of the ISS were built in different parts of the world, and they were then connected in space like a LEGO set by robots and humans. The ISS is as long as an American football field. There are six sleeping quarters, two bathrooms, and a gym—plus a bay window with a 360-degree view of Earth! Every day it travels the equivalent of a trip to the moon and back.

Fun Fact: In 2009, 13 people were aboard the ISS at one time. That's the record for most people in space!

The ISS orbits the earth every 90 minutes. At night, it can be seen with the naked eye without any special equipment—it's usually the brightest object in the sky besides the moon. If you spot it, know that seven people are probably on board at any given time. Incredible!

224 One World Trade Center: Onward & Upward

More than 13 years after the 9/11 tragedy, One World Trade Center opened in New York City. It's the tallest building in the United States and in the western hemisphere, but the seventh tallest in the world. It stands at 1,776 feet (541 m)—a direct reference to the year the Declaration of Independence was signed. That number includes the 408-foot (124 m) spire on top.

One World Trade Center has 71 elevators that can travel as fast as 23 miles per hour (37 km/hr). That means it takes just 60 seconds to go from the ground floor to the 102nd floor. You can visit the three-level observation deck on the top floors to see stunning views of New York City.

225 Ice Bucket Challenge: A Viral Sensation

In the summer of 2014, people loved dumping buckets of ice water over their heads and then challenging a friend to do the same. It was part of a viral fundraising campaign that spread like crazy over social media with the hashtag #ALSIceBucketChallenge, which helped raise money to fight against ALS. ALS is short for amyotrophic lateral sclerosis, which is a disease that affects nerve cells in the brain and spinal cord.

Celebrities like LeBron James, Lady Gaga, Taylor Swift, and Selena Gomez joined in. President Barack Obama was challenged but politely declined—he donated money instead. In 2022, a new drug for ALS was approved, and it was funded directly from the ALS Ice Bucket Challenge.

226 **Marriage Equality for All:** Same Sex Marriage is Legal

On June 26, 2015, the Supreme Court ruled on a case called *Obergefell v. Hodges*—it made it legal for same-sex couples to marry in all 50 states. President Barack Obama called the ruling, "A victory for America." It was considered a major step forward for civil rights, specifically gay rights.

The fight for marriage equality began in the 1990s. Before the Supreme Court ruling, different states had different laws about same-sex marriages—some allowed them while others banned them. The decision overturned the bans in 13 states and gave same-sex married couples the same rights as straight married couples, which includes access to their partner's health care plans, financial benefits like filing their taxes together, and being legally recognized as a child's parent.

227 **Hillary Clinton:** One Step Closer to the First Female President

Ninety-five years after women secured the right to vote, former Secretary of State, First Lady, and Senator Hillary Rodham Clinton added one more title to her list: presidential candidate. Clinton became the first woman to secure a nomination for president, which meant she was running for president as a Democrat in 2016. Clinton won the support of almost 66 million Americans, but she ultimately ended up losing the race to Republican nominee Donald J. Trump.

Clinton was the first First Lady elected to the US Senate. Her husband was former president Bill Clinton, who held office from 1993 to 2001. She was also the first woman elected to a statewide office in New York. In her career, Clinton helped rebuild New York after 9/11, championed affordable health care, and fought for women's rights. Clinton went on to become the author of many best-selling books, including some for kids which she coauthored with her daughter Chelsea.

228 Hamilton the Musical: Rewriting History

Hamilton, a hip-hop musical based on the life of Alexander Hamilton (page 24), took the world of Broadway by storm when it debuted in the summer of 2015. It was created by Puerto Rican American composer, playwright, and actor Lin-Manuel Miranda, who also starred in the musical as Hamilton.

Miranda mixed modern hip-hop with 1700s history. He cast diverse actors to play the roles of the founding men and women who built America—who historically were all white. The catchy and clever lyrics managed to share the story of our country, but with a modern melody that will forever hold a place in pop culture history.

In June of 2016, it was no surprise when, after being nominated for a record 16 Tony Awards, *Hamilton* won 11—just shy of the record of 12 awards. All four of the performance-based Tony Awards went to Black actors, three of them from *Hamilton*: Reneé Elise Goldberry, Daveed Diggs, and Leslie Odom Jr.

Miranda had already gotten some fame and awards for his first musical, *In the Heights*, which featured his Latino neighborhood in New York City. Miranda is an EGOT winner, which means he has won an Emmy, Grammy, Oscar, and Tony for his various projects, as well as a 2016 Pulitzer Prize for *Hamilton*.

229 The Cubs Win the World Series: The Curse Is Broken!

In November of 2016, the Chicago Cubs won the World Series for the first time in 108 years, which ended the longest championship drought in North American sports history and the longest World Series drought in baseball history. The last time they had won a World Series was when they beat the Detroit Tigers in back-to-back championships in 1907 and 1908. That's when cars were being invented!

The Cubs beat the Cleveland Guardians 8–7 during a suspenseful and rainy game seven of the Series at Wrigley Field in Chicago. The win broke the "Billy Goat Curse," one of the most famous sports curses, which was allegedly placed on the team in 1945 by the owner of the Billy Goat Tavern. He and his goat Murphy, who he brought for good luck, were denied entry into Wrigley Field during the World Series. He had even bought Murphy a ticket! The Cubs lost the game that night and the Series—and they never won another World Series again. Until 2016.

230 Plastic Bag Ban: California Says No to Plastic Bags

The average time of use for a plastic bag is 12 minutes—things need to change. In 2016, California became the first state to ban single-use plastic bags from stores. While the law banned thin shopping bags, it allowed people to buy thicker plastic bags. People still barely reused or recycled them. To fix this, California Governor Gavin Newsom made a new law in 2024 that banned all plastic bags completely by 2026. Only recycled paper or compostable bags will be allowed for takeout food or checkout lines.

Advocacy groups hope that California's plastic problem will finally improve with this new change. The plastic bag ban has made waves in the US—more than ever, people are aware of the plastic they use, like straws (many are now paper straws or compostable) or plastic storage containers. There's a lot more work to do when it comes to being environmentally conscious, but using a tote or a reusable grocery bag is a step in the right direction.

Women's March on Washington:
America's Largest Single-Day Protest

On January 21, 2017, millions of people marched in every state across the country to draw attention to women's rights. In New York City, 400,000 people marched up Fifth Avenue. In Los Angeles, 750,000 marched through downtown. And in Washington, DC, hundreds of thousands of people crowded the capital.

The Women's March movement took place on the first full day President Donald J. Trump took office. Protesters believed he made statements that were anti-woman during his 2016 presidential campaign and feared he was a threat to human rights. They fought for racial equality, LGBTQIA+ rights, health care reform, and religious freedom too.

Many people (and many celebrities) wore pink and marched through the streets of cities around the United States. They carried signs and posters that said, "Girls just want to have fundamental rights," and shared images of Princess Leia from *Star Wars*, who is a symbol of the resistance. The peaceful protests sparked a movement, and the Women's March Network continues to organize events and advocate for women today.

232 Mirai Nagasu: Landing the Impossible at the Olympics

During the 2018 Winter Olympics in Korea, Japanese American figure skater Mirai Nagasu became the first American woman to land a triple axel jump in an Olympic competition.

A triple axel is one of the most difficult and dangerous tricks in figure skating. It's the only time a skater jumps forward into the air. They must rotate three and a half times in less than a second before landing backward. No other skaters even attempted to plant the triple axel jump that day. Nagasu went on to earn the second highest score—it helped that a triple axel was worth twice the points of a double axel!

233 The Center of a Universe: Black Hole Captured

In April of 2019, astronomers captured the first image of a black hole—something that had once been a mystery. Now Albert Einstein's theory of relativity from 1916, which discussed how gravity, space, and time affected each other, could be proven. A black hole is thought to be a collapse of massive stars, and it leaves a hole with a gravitational pull so strong that not even light can escape it.

This black hole is located at the center of a galaxy called Messier 87, about 55 million light years from Earth (a light year is the distance light travels in one year, which is almost six trillion miles [ten trillion km]). Our galaxy, the Milky Way, also has a black hole at the center.

234 Self-Driving Cars: Robotaxis Arrive in Arizona

Hop in a car. Now imagine there's no one in the driver's seat and the steering wheel moves by itself! Waymo, which started as a secret Google project, launched its "robotaxi" service in October of 2020 to passengers in Arizona.

Driverless vehicles have the potential to make the roads safer for everyone. They're equipped with cameras and sensors that give them an instant 360-degree view as they drive and allow them to anticipate things around them—much faster than a human ever could.

235

President Trump: Operation Warp Speed

After the World Health Organization declared the COVID-19 virus a global pandemic in March of 2020, President Donald J. Trump came up with a plan to ensure the United States had a vaccine to fight against the virus—as fast as possible. The Trump Administration called it Operation Warp Speed, and they hoped to create a vaccine within months even though developing a vaccine usually took years.

COVID-19 cases continued to climb around the world, but on December 14, a vaccine had finally arrived. The first shot was given to a nurse in New York, then to other Americans around the country who needed to protect themselves as they cared for those who were infected. By January 2021, one million Americans were getting vaccinated every day. Operation Warp Speed was the most urgent mass immunization effort since the polio vaccine in the 1950s.

236

Skin Tone Crayons: Crayola Thinks Outside the Box

In 2020, Crayola did something it had never done before. It released a "Colors of the World" pack of 24 crayons that represents different skin tones from around the world from light to deep shades. That means kids of all skin tones could more accurately color drawings of themselves—instead of trying to mix two shades that didn't really look like their skin.

Experts at Crayola partnered with makeup chemists from the beauty industry to create the perfect shades. The "Colors of the World" line of crayons was a huge success and went on to include markers and colored pencils in different skin tones too.

JoAnne S. Bass: The Military's Highest-Ranking Female

When JoAnne S. Bass became the 19th Chief Master Sergeant of the US Air Force in 2020, she made history twice. She was the first woman and first Asian American person to hold the highest senior enlisted level of leadership in any military branch.

Bass grew up as a military kid and lived on military bases in the US and overseas before she joined the Air Force in 1993. She completed basic training, which is an intense seven-week-long boot camp, at Joint Base in San Antonio, Texas. She only planned on staying in the Air Force for four years, but she soon realized that serving in the Air Force meant that she was supporting a cause greater than herself.

During her time in the Air Force, she held leadership positions and gained experience across the US and overseas. She even worked at the Pentagon in Washington, DC, which is the headquarters of the US Department of Defense. As Chief Master Sergeant, Bass oversaw more than 600,000 airmen and made sure they were happy, healthy, and well-trained. Bass retired from her position on March 8, 2024, and she now serves as a board member for the Military Women's Memorial, a monument and exhibit in Arlington, Virginia, that acts as a tribute to women who have served in the military throughout history. As of 2023, women made up 21 percent of the Air Force.

238 Kamala Harris: "We Did It, Joe."

After President Joe Biden's 2020 election win, Kamala Harris became the first woman to serve as vice president, making her the highest-ranking female official in US history. Two other women had previously run for vice president, but their teams hadn't won the election. Harris also became the first Black American and the first Asian American to hold the position. (Her father immigrated from Jamaica and her mother from India.) When she took office, her husband, Doug Emhoff, became the very first Second Gentleman.

Harris ran for president in the 2024 presidential election against former President Trump (now the 45th and 47th president). She ultimately lost the race but inspired a generation of women, which she highlighted in her concession speech. She encouraged Americans to never give up and always keep fighting.

239 Tom Brady: "GOAT" Quarterback

When the Tampa Bay Buccaneers beat the Kansas City Chiefs 31–9 at the 55th Super Bowl in 2021, quarterback Tom Brady picked up yet another ring—his seventh to be exact, which is more than any other player in NFL history. He set another record while doing it: At age 43, he became the oldest player to ever compete in a Super Bowl.

Brady played for the New England Patriots for 20 seasons, and he played in nine Super Bowl games as a Patriot. When he left for the Buccaneers, fans were shocked. He ended up retiring in 2022—changing his mind 40 days later—and played one more season (his third for the Buccaneers) before finally retiring for good. He's often called the "GOAT," which stands for greatest of all time.

240

Juneteenth: Celebrating Freedom for Black Americans

In 2021, Juneteenth became an official national holiday, but it's tied to a fateful day more than 150 years ago.

During the Civil War on January 1, 1863, President Abraham Lincoln signed the Emancipation Proclamation (page 40). It ended slavery in the Confederate states. Though enslaved people in the South were technically now free, they weren't immediately freed. News was slow to reach certain states, and some enslavers and white people tried to hide the news.

Fun Fact: Juneteenth is the twelfth federal holiday, and the first one to be introduced since Martin Luther King, Jr. Day in 1983.

It was up to the Union troops from the North to enforce the new law. Back then, the army traveled by foot, wagon, or horseback—and Texas was the furthest Southern state. Almost two years later, on June 19, 1865, thousands of Union soldiers marched into Galveston Bay, Texas, and announced that the enslaved people in Texas were freed.

The newly freed people called the day "Juneteenth" or "Freedom Day." Finally, in December of that year, the 13th Amendment, which abolished slavery nationwide, was ratified, or made official in the US Constitution.

Today, Black Americans celebrate Juneteenth with parades, barbecues, and family gatherings. The holiday represents the fight for human rights and the progress that has been made.

241 "Quad King": Nathan Chen Wins Gold

At the Winter Olympics of 2022 in China, figure skater Nathan Chen did the impossible: He landed *five* separate quadruple jumps (that's a jump with four turns!) in his free skate program. His performance to a medley of Elton John songs went on to secure him the gold medal for Team USA. He earned a record-breaking 332.6 combined points for his short program and free skate—22 points ahead of his competitor in a sport that usually comes down to the decimal! At the previous 2018 Olympics, Chen did not perform well and came in 17th place. His huge 2022 comeback inspired others to never give up.

242 Zero Car Emissions by 2035: Clean Air for All

In California, car fumes are the largest source of air pollution—about 80 percent of the state's pollution can be attributed to the high number of gas-guzzling cars on the road. But in 2022, California passed the Advanced Clean Cars II rule to fix this problem. The rule includes year-by-year goals that start in 2026 and end in 2035 when all new cars sold in California must be hybrid or electric cars. California was the first state to pass this kind of rule, and 11 more states are following in their footsteps.

243 ChatGPT: How Can I Help You?

When an early version of ChatGPT, a chatbot run by artificial intelligence (AI), was released in November of 2022, it went viral—fast. Five days later, over one million users were testing out ChatGPT. Users could ask the chatbot a question, and it would respond with a very helpful, or not so helpful, answer. It's kind of like googling something, but you don't have to click on links to read more—ChatGPT can write it all out for you in a conversational way. Users started asking it to plan their upcoming trips, write recipes, code computer programs, or even draft up original songs. Some people love ChatGPT and others hate it for its environmental impacts (training AI requires a *lot* of electricity).

244 **The Eras Tour:** It's Taylor Swift's World

Pop star Taylor Swift opened her concert tour in Arizona in March of 2023, but this wasn't just any tour. The Eras Tour would go on to become the first concert tour to make over $1 billion in ticket sales. As the tour continued, it crossed the $2 billion mark—double the amount of any other tour ever.

Her fans, known as "Swifties," watched her take the stage for over nearly two years across 51 cities, 21 countries, and five continents. Swifties became known for their joy, passion, and friendship bracelet trading. Swift became known for her nonstop energy—and her sparkly high-heeled boots. She performed 149 sold-out shows (more than three hours each) over about 630 days, including a record eight shows at Wembley Stadium in England.

Fun Fact: At the Seattle concert in July of 2023, Swifties danced so hard during "Shake it Off" that they created the equivalent of a 2.4-magnitude earthquake.

During the tour, Swift released three albums: rerecorded versions of *1989* and *Speak Now*, which are "Taylor's Version," plus a new album called *The Tortured Poets Department*. She became Spotify's most-streamed artist for two years in a row. Her concert had turned into a worldwide pop culture phenomenon. She even turned her tour into a movie! *Taylor Swift: The Eras Tour* is now considered the most successful concert film of all time.

Swift started breaking records when she was just 17 years old. With her single, "Our Song," she became the youngest artist in history to have written and performed a song that was number one on the Hot Country Songs chart. She's now the artist with the most American Music Awards in history—40 awards. The previous record holder had 26!

245 Rubik's Cube Record: Solved in Seconds

At the age of 21, Max Park solved a Rubik's Cube in less than a minute on June 11, 2023. In fact, he solved the cube-shaped puzzle in seconds—3.13 seconds. Park broke the previous 3x3 record time by a fraction of a second.

Park was diagnosed with autism as a toddler. He had trouble unscrewing the cap of a water bottle, so his mother thought that a Rubik's Cube could be a great way to improve his finger and hand strength. Now a world champion, Park has quicker fingers than most!

Park is considered a "speedcuber," or a person who competes quickly to solve puzzles like a Rubik's Cube. There are over 140,000 cubers from 140 countries registered in the speedcubers community. Sometimes the competitors solve pyramid-shaped cubes, wear blindfolds, and solve the puzzles with one hand. They're competitive, nail-biting competitions!

246 Solar Eclipse: Don't Look!

Around lunchtime on a Monday in April of 2024, millions of Americans turned their heads to the sky—wearing special glasses, of course. It was a rare total solar eclipse that was sweeping across the country. As the moon passed in front of the sun, it created total darkness in the middle of the day. The eclipse couldn't be viewed with a naked eye except for the moments of darkness when the moon was completely blocking the sun.

People traveled for hours to get to specific locations on the path of "totality," which means they could witness moments of total darkness when the sunshine was completely blocked. (Other parts of the country only witnessed a partial eclipse.) The crowds gathered to observe the unique natural phenomenon that only lasted three and a half to four minutes, depending on where they were viewing it. Another solar eclipse won't happen in the US until 2044.

247 **Beyoncé:** *Cowboy Carter* Wins!

At the 52nd annual Grammy Awards in 2010, Beyoncé won six Grammys, which was the year of her hit song, "Single Ladies (Put A Ring On It)" and her album *I Am . . . Sascha Fierce*. She was the first female artist to win that many awards in one night.

Beyoncé started singing at age seven and rose to fame as one of three members of the 1990s R&B group, Destiny's Child, before starting her own solo career in 2003. Beyoncé is no stranger to setting records, which is why her fans gave her the nickname "Queen Bey." At the 2023 Grammy Awards, Beyoncé had already tied with her husband, hip-hop artist Jay-Z, for the most Grammy nominations ever—but then she won four more. That made Beyoncé the artist with the most Grammys of all time (male or female) with 32 awards . . . and she now has 35.

In 2024, she made history again when she became the first Black woman to top the Billboard country album charts with *Act II: Cowboy Carter*. Beyoncé finally won best album at the 2025 Grammy Awards as well as best country album—much to Beyoncé's evident surprise at the award ceremony. Billboard named Beyoncé the greatest pop star of the twenty-first century.

Steph Curry: "Golden Dagger" at the Olympics

Team USA may have won four straight Olympic golds for basketball prior to 2024, but Paris 2024 was Steph Curry's Games debut. As the point guard for the Golden State Warriors, Curry is no stranger to medals and trophies. A ten-time All-NBA player, four-time NBA Champion, and ten-time NBA All-Star—to name a few—Curry is considered one of the greatest point guards of all time.

Curry's "Golden Dagger" shot was his eighth and final three-pointer in the final against France. He described it as the best three-pointer in his career after a flurry of shots in a nail-biting game. Four of the eight three-pointers were in the last three minutes of the game, taking the score up to 98–87 for Team USA.

Simone Biles: The Most Decorated Gymnast in History

At the 2024 Paris Olympics, gymnast Simone Biles scored her eighth Olympic medal when Team USA won gold—and that made her the most decorated Olympic gymnast in history! Biles went on to earn three more medals: two golds for all-around and vault and a silver for floor. Now her Olympic medal count sits at 11—and seven are gold!

At only four feet eight inches tall, Biles can jump as high as 12 feet (4 m) during her floor routines. And she has five different gymnastics moves named after her like the Biles II, which includes two flips and three twists. It seems like her skills defy physics, but her strength and speed allow her to do incredible moves on the floor and on the vault, where she gets a little help flying high from a springboard.

250 Pope Leo XIV: First American Pope . . . Ever

On May 8, 2025, Cardinal Robert Francis Prevost was elected to be the 267th head of the Catholic church, taking the name Pope Leo XIV. Each pope changes their name when they're elected to show what they hope to achieve as the pope. There is a long line of Pope Leos that Pope Leo XIV looks up to. By taking their name, the pope hopes to honor them through his own service.

Fun Fact: The pope lives in Vatican City, the smallest country in the world. It's even smaller than New York City's Central Park!

Pope Leo XIV is the first pope from the United States—many have been from Italy. Leo was born in Chicago in 1955. He went to seminary, which is a religious school to prepare to serve the church, and he also studied mathematics at Villanova University in Pennsylvania. A pope can be many things!

While Leo is American, he spent 20 years in Peru as a bishop, archbishop, then cardinal. These years prepared him for his papacy, or being the pope. The pope values prayer, charity, and service to people around the world. The priority of the pope is to connect with people and spread kindness.

A new pope is selected after the death of the last pope. Then, the extremely secretive process called the conclave begins. Cardinals meet in Vatican City to select the next pope by anonymously voting amongst themselves. During this two-to-three-day period, Catholics wait to see white smoke come out of the Sistine Chapel—this means over a billion Catholics have their new pope!

Glossary

AAPI: An acronym that stands for Asian American and Pacific Islander. This is a term for any person descended from Asia or the Pacific Islands.

abolish: To formally put an end to something.

advertising: Promoting something (like a product or service) to an audience in hopes that they buy it.

aerospace: An industry that makes aircraft, which are vehicles that fly through the air (like planes) or space (like satellites).

agriculture: The science of farming, which includes growing crops (like fruits and vegetables) and raising animals (like cows and chickens) to produce food.

arcade: Short for video arcade, where coin-operated video game consoles (including pinball machines and claw machines) can be played by gamers.

armistice: An agreement between two opposing sides to stop fighting a war.

artificial intelligence (AI): The ability for a computer to process information and problem-solve almost like it has human intelligence.

assassinate: To kill someone important, like a political figure, for a political reason.

astronaut: Someone who travels to space for work; they can be scientists, pilots, or engineers.

aviation: The science of flying and designing aircraft, like planes and helicopters.

ban: A rule that says something is not allowed.

black hole: An invisible hole in space where gravity is so strong that even light cannot get out.

boycott: A type of protest where people agree to stop buying something or going somewhere to make a point and bring about change.

Broadway: A theater district in New York City that's named after a portion of Broadway Street, where many of the theaters are located.

CEO: The top person in charge of a company. It stands for Chief Executive Officer.

CGI: Using computers to create pictures and special effects for movies, games, and TV shows. It stands for computer-generated imagery.

civil rights: A set of rules that make sure every citizen is treated the same way and has the same opportunities regardless of race, gender, or religion.

colony: When people (called colonists) from one country settle in a new place in a different country but still follow the rules of their original country, or a country or area under the control of a distant country and occupied by settlers.

commemorate: To honor the memory of something with a special item or ceremony.

Congress: A group of elected leaders who makes laws for the US. A congressman or congresswoman is one member of that team.

conservationist: Someone who protects nature, like oceans and forests, and the animals that live in them.

constitution: A set of rules and laws that explain the rights of the people and how a government works. It's the highest law in the US.

debate: A conversation where people share their opinion on a subject and try to explain why their viewpoint is better.

democracy: A type of government where people have the power to vote and choose their leaders. It means "rule by the people" in Greek.

discrimination: Treating someone differently or unfairly because of their race, gender, religion, or something else that makes them different.

eclipse: When one object in space (like the moon or Earth) passes in front of another object (like the sun) and blocks its light.

EGOT: When a person wins all four awards in the entertainment industry: Emmy (TV), Grammy (music), Oscar (film), and Tony (theater).

emission: Gases or substances that are released into the air, often from cars.

endangered species: Animals or plants that are at risk of disappearing from the earth . . . forever.

engineer: Someone who designs and builds machines, buildings, and more. An engineering marvel is something impressive that they created.

enlist: To join the military.

entrepreneur: A person who starts and runs their own business.

fossil: An imprint on a rock or the preserved leftovers of an ancient plant or animal, like footprints, bones, teeth, or shells.

GOAT: An acronym that stands for "Greatest of All Time," which is used to describe someone who is the best in their field.

GPS: Using signals from satellites to determine a person's location. It's an acronym that stands for Global Positioning System.

Grammy: A music industry award given to singers, musicians, and songwriters.

gross: The total amount of money that something makes before subtracting the expenses (what it cost to make it).

hashtag: The pound sign (#) with a word or phrase attached. They're used to tag popular topics on social media.

hippie: A nickname for people in the 1960s and 1970s who advocated for peace and love instead of war and discrimination.

immigrant: A person who moves from one country to live in another.

mint: A place where money, like coins and paper bills, are made.

monument: A statue or building that honors a person or event.

NAACP: An organization that fights for equal rights for all African Americans.

national park: Areas of nature in the US that are protected for people to visit and explore.

negotiate: When two or more parties talk things through until they find a fair solution that everyone agrees on.

New World: A term early European explorers used for the Americas.

Olympics: A competition in which athletes from around the world compete for gold, silver, and bronze medals. Someone who competes in the Olympics is called an Olympian or an Olympic athlete.

Oscar: Also called an Academy Award, the top award given for movies.

papacy: When a religious leader, known as the pope, rules the Catholic Church.

patent: An official document that protects someone's idea or invention so they are the only one who can make it or sell it.

pilgrim: A person who traveled to a new land seeking religious freedom.

plantation: A large farm, often found in the South before the Civil War, where enslaved people worked and tended to the crops.

point guard: The leader of the basketball team who is in charge of the team's offensive plays and helps others score.

president: The elected leader of a country.

Presidential Medal of Freedom: A special award given by the president of the US to people who have done something great for the country.

protest: When people gather or speak out to show they disapprove of something or someone.

radio: A way of sending sound or information (like music or news) through the air, which is then played on a speaker.

ratify: To officially approve a new law so that it can go into effect.

rebel: A person who stands up for what they believe in by going against the government or leader who they believe is unfair.

redcoat: A nickname for British soldiers that fought in the Revolutionary War.

reservation: Land set aside by the government for a certain group of people, like Native American tribes, where they can live and abide by their own rules and laws.

resource: Something useful found in nature, like water, trees, or energy.

revolution: A big change in a government or a way of living that usually involves rebels, fighting, and/or a war.

Roaring Twenties: The period of the 1920s in the US known for jazz music, dancing, and other fun hobbies that people finally had time for.

rover: A remote-controlled robotic vehicle that explores the surface of planets, like Mars, and sends information back to Earth.

satellite: A machine that is launched into space to orbit Earth to take photos (which can help predict weather) or direct TV signals and long-distance phone calls.

segregation: Unfairly separating people into different groups or areas based on their race.

senator: A person who is elected to the US Senate, which helps make laws for the government.

slavery: An unfair system in which people were owned by other people and forced to work without pay.

speaker of the house: The leader of the US House of Representatives, one of the two parts of Congress that help make laws for the country.

suffragist: A woman who fought for the right to vote in the late 1800s and early 1900s. Men also supported the cause, but the suffrage movement was mostly made up of women.

Super Bowl: The final championship game of the NFL (National Football League)

Supreme Court: The highest court in the US that makes the final decision about important laws and the meaning of the Constitution.

tax: A way for the government to collect money from people and businesses which can then be used to pay for things that everyone needs, like libraries, roads, and schools.

Tejano: A style of music that blends Mexican and American sounds.

telegraph: A message that was sent over wires using electric signals and a code, which was then decoded and read. This was a way to communicate before telephones.

***Titanic*:** The largest ship of its time that tragically sank in 1912 after hitting an iceberg, making it the most famous shipwreck in history.

tribe: A group of people from the same community who share the same culture and language, especially Native American groups.

Underground Railroad: A secret system of safehouses that helped enslaved people escape from the southern US to find freedom in the North and in Canada.

United Nations: An organization made up of countries around the world who have pledged to work together and help keep the peace.

veteran: Someone who has served in a branch of the military, like the Army, Air Force, Navy, Marine Corp, Coast Guard, or Space Force.

vice president: The second-highest elected leader in the US government.

vinyl: A round, flat disc, often called a "record," used to play music on a record player.

World's Fair: A big, temporary event held in a city where countries around the world set up exhibits to showcase their latest culture, art, and inventions.

Index

IMAGE CREDITS: PAGE 4 Manu Cunhas **PAGE 6** Manu Cunhas **PAGE 10** Shutterstock.com **PAGE 12** Manu Cunhas **PAGE 13** Culture Club / Hulton Archive / Getty Images **PAGE 14** Royalty-free / Moment / Getty Images **PAGE 16** Shawshots / Alamy Stock Photo **PAGE 17** GraphicaArtis / Archive Photos / Getty Images **PAGE 18** Heritage Images / Hulton Archive/ Getty Images **PAGE 19** Shutterstock.com **PAGE 20** Hulton Archive /Getty Images **PAGE 22** Hulton Archive /Getty Images **PAGE 23** Library of Congress / Corbis Historical / Getty Images **PAGE 24** Shutterstock.com **PAGE 26** Manu Cunhas **PAGE 27** Shutterstock.com **PAGE 28** North Wind Picture Archives / Alamy Stock Photo **PAGE 30** Piemags / library / Alamy Stock Photo **PAGE 31** Historical / Corbis Historical / Getty Images **PAGE 32** Shutterstock.com **PAGE 33** Shutterstock.com **PAGE 34** John Elk III / Alamy Stock Photo **PAGE 35** Pictorial Press Ltd / Alamy Stock Photo **PAGE 36** Benjamin F. Powelson, Photographer, Library of Congress Prints and Photographs Division Washington, D.C. **PAGE 37** Sheridan Libraries / Levy / Gado / Archive Photos / Getty Images **PAGE 38** Shutterstock.com **PAGE 40** Shutterstock.com **PAGE 42** Culture Club / Hulton Archive / Getty Images **PAGE 43** Paul Harris / Archive Photos / Getty Images **PAGE 44** Shutterstock.com **PAGE 46** Shutterstock.com **PAGE 47** Above: Photographs in Carol M. Highsmith's America Project in the Carol M. Highsmith Archive, Library of Congress, Prints and Photographs Division Below: Palmquist & Jurgens, photographer / Library of Congress, Prints and Photographs Division **PAGE 48** Shutterstock.com **PAGE 49** Shutterstock.com **PAGE 50** Science & Society Picture Library / SSPL / Getty Images **PAGE 51** Bettmann / Getty Images **PAGE 52** Shutterstock.com **PAGE 53** Shutterstock.com **PAGE 54** Manu Cunhas **PAGE 55** World History Archive / Alamy Stock Photo **PAGE 56** Shutterstock.com **PAGE 57** Shutterstock.com **PAGE 58** Shutterstock.com **PAGE 59** LandlordsGame.Info / Wikipedia **PAGE 61** Jakub Sisulak / Shutterstock.com **PAGE 62** Chizhevskaya Ekaterina / Shuuerstock.com **PAGE 63** P Russell Lee, photographer / Library of Congress Prints and Photographs Division Washington, D.C. 20540 USA **PAGE 64** Shutterstock.com **PAGE 65** Shutterstock.com **PAGE 66** Hulton Deutsch / Corbis Historical / Getty Images **PAGE 67** Harris & Ewing, photographer / Library of Congress Prints and Photographs Division Washington, D.C. 20540 USA **PAGE 68** Michael Ochs Archives / Stringer **PAGE 69** Scott Olson / Getty Images **PAGE 70** Oklahoma Historical Society / Archive photos / Getty Images **PAGE 71** Getty Images **PAGE 72** Bettmann / Getty Images **PAGE 73** Larry Prock / Shutterstock.com **PAGE 74** Shutterstock.com **PAGE 74** Louis Van Oeyen/ WRHS / Getty Images **PAGE 75** Louis Van Oeyen/ WRHS / Getty Images 76 Shutterstock.com **PAGE 77** Interim Archives / Getty Images **PAGE 78** Interim Archives / Getty Images **PAGE 79** Shutterstock.com **PAGE 80** Stock Montage / Archive Photos / Getty Images **PAGE 81** Shutterstock.com **PAGE 82** Allstar Picture Library Ltd / Amamy Stock Photo **PAGE 84** Shutterstock.com **PAGE 85** PhotoQuest / Archive Photos / Getty Images **PAGE 86** Shawshots / Alamy Stock Photo **PAGE 87** New York Daily News Archive /Getty Images **PAGE 88**Shutterstock.com **PAGE 89** Bettmann / Getty Images **PAGE 90** Shutterstock.com **PAGE 91** Don Cravens / The Chronicle Collection / Getty Images **PAGE 92** Michael Ochs Archives / Stringer / Getty Images **PAGE 93**New York Times Co. / Archive Photos / Getty Images **PAGE 94** Interim Archives / Getty Images **PAGE 96** Yvonne Hemsey / Hulton Archive / Getty Images **PAGE 99** Photo by AFP / Getty Images **PAGE 100** Bachrach / Archive Photos / Getty Images **PAGE 101** Keystone Press / Alamy Stock Photo **PAGE 102** Silver Screen Collection / Getty Images **PAGE 103** Bettmann / Getty Images **PAGE 104** Shutterstock.com **PAGE 105** Shutterstock.com **PAGE 106** Entertainment Pictures / Alamy Stock Photo **PAGE 107** Collection Christophel / Alamy Stock Photo **PAGE 109** Niday Picture Library / Alamy Stock Photo **PAGE 110** Shutterstock.com **PAGE 111** Bettmann / Getty Images **PAGE 112** Shutterstock.com **PAGE 113** BFA / Alamy Stock Photo **PAGE 114** FlixPix / Alamy Stock Photo **PAGE 116** Phil Rees / Alamy Stock Photo **PAGE 118** Steve Powell / Getty Images **PAGE 120** Interim Archives / Getty Images **PAGE 122** Photology1971 / Shutterstock.com **PAGE 123** AFP / Getty Images **PAGE 124** Donaldson Collection / Michael Ochs Archives / Getty Images **PAGE 125** Paragon Sneakers / Shutterstock.com **PAGE 127** Pictorial Press Ltd / Alamy Stock Photo **PAGE 129** Arlene Richie / The Chronicle Collection / Getty Images **PAGE 130** Shutterstock.com **PAGE 131** Wirestock Creators / Shutterstock.com **PAGE 132** Maximum Film / Alamy Stock Photo **PAGE 133** PCN Photography / Alamy Stock Photo **PAGE 134** Eugene Gologursky / Stringer / Getty Images **PAGE 136** Manu Cunhas **PAGE 137** Camerique / Archive Photos / Getty Images **PAGE 138** DFree / Shutterstock.com **PAGE 140** True Images / Alamy Stock Image **PAGE 141** Thomas J. Peterson / Alamy Stock Photo **PAGE 142** Kim Kulish / Corbis Historical / Getty Images **PAGE 144** Octavio Hoyos / Shutterstock.com **PAGE 146** Storms Media Group / Alamy Stock Photo **PAGE 147** LWM/NASA/LANDSAT/Alamy Stock Photo **PAGE 148** Boston Globe / Getty Images **PAGE 149** Anthony Correia / Shutterstock.com **PAGE 150** WENN Rights Ltd / Alamy Stock Photo **PAGE 151** Shutterstock.com **PAGE 152** G. Midford / Shutterstock.com **PAGE 153** NASA's Scientific Visualization Studio - Krystofer Kim, Jeremy Schnittman, Francis Reddy, Jeremy Schnittman, Scott Wiessinger, Sophia Roberts **PAGE 154** Lynn Watson / Shutterstock.com **PAGE 155** Operation 2021 / Alamy Stock Photo **PAGE 156** Andrew Leyden / Shutterstock.com **PAGE 157** Anadolu / Getty Images **PAGE 158** Olga Besnard / Shutterstock.com **PAGE 159** Brian Friedman / Shutterstock.com **PAGE 160** NASA/Joel Kowsky **PAGE 161** Kevin Winter / Getty Images **PAGE 162** Gregory Shamus / Getty Images **PAGE 163** Marco Iacobucci Epp / Shutterstock.com **PAGE 169** Shutterstock.com

Acknowledgments

A big thank-you to my editors Nicole James and Sarah O'Connor for helping me distill 250 years of history into one book—no easy feat!

About the Author

Aubre Andrus is the award-winning author of The Look Up Series, a women in STEM career series for kids, plus more than 50 books published by National Geographic Kids, Scholastic, Lonely Planet Kids, Disney, American Girl, and more. She lives in Los Angeles with her husband and daughters.